Astrology And Enneagram

Understanding And Finding Yourself Through Astrology and Enneagram (Zodiac Signs, Horoscopes, Personality Types, Spiritual Growth, Self Awareness, Spirituality)

Alex Fletcher

Astrology

Finding Yourself And Others Through Horoscopes And The 12 Zodiac Signs For Spiritual Growth, Personality Awareness and Self Discovery

© Copyright 2018 - All rights reserved.

It is not legal to reproduce, duplicate, or transmit any part of this document in either electronic means or in printed format. Recording of this publication is strictly prohibited and any storage of this document is not allowed unless with written permission from the publisher except for the use of brief quotations in a book review.

Table Of Content

Introduction 1
Chapter 1: The 12 Zodiac Signs 3
Chapter 2 Relationship Astrology: 65
Chapter 3: Finding Yourself through Your Zodiac and Growing on a Spiritual Level 76
Chapter 4: How You Can Strengthen Your Relationships and Friendships by Reading the Zodiac Signs 83
Chapter 5: Birthday Charts 96
Chapter 6: Astrology and the 12 Cell Salts 98
Chapter 7: Extra Information 107
Conclusion 121

Introduction

Your journey may have started with "What is a horoscope?" and "What is my sign?" Astrology is such an interesting topic that just seems to make sense when we read or listen to the traits that come with our specific star sign. Due to the substantial amount of agreement within the population when compared to their zodiac sign, it comes to the point where Horoscopes are quite certainly real. And it is at this moment we realize and accept that we can actually take advantage of our star signs according to you own self and life and even the friendships or relationships we have with others!

This book provides powerful information and allows you to find personality traits that will guide you down the path towards investigating all that you can find using Astrology.

That horoscope or map that appears as a two dimensional chart showing the position of the planets, Moon, and Sun, at the precise moment of when you were born is just the beginning. A thorough horoscope, also known as a natal chart, astrology chart, or the birth chart, can be thought of like the instructions for the hand you have been dealt in this life.

However, following this does not suggest that your life has already been decided. It is largely up to you to decide what you follow and the changes you make based on what your horoscope can tell you. Even given your freedom of choice, your horoscope reflects the natural inclinations you have, your issues to be faced, any lessons you have to learn, and the problems you may have to solve. It may be used as an abstract formula showing the energies you possess or perhaps obstacles you have been tasked with.

This book is about the positives of yours and others star signs and how you can use them to your advantage!

Astrology can provide you with information allowing it to be a popular key towards understanding yourself and those around you, but it probably won't provide concrete, clear, or simple answers to your problems. Using the information in your horoscope might give you understanding and insight into the reasons you behave as you do. If you research the horoscope of the people you deal with on a regular basis, you may have a better understanding of the actions of friends, family, or lovers. This can lead to better acceptance, patience, and tolerance of interactions.

The zodiac and the theory of astrology believe mankind is not only influenced by hereditary factors, life experiences, and their environment, but also by the very solar system at the moment. The planets are viewed as life-forces and these planetary forces take on different aspects, depending on their zodiacal position and how they relate to each another. By reading the roles of the planets, the elements, the signs, and the houses, they create a comprehensive reading. Astrology presents a picture of a person and their potential based on a birth chart. When you have the the sun, the moon or a planet in a particular sign, then the qualities of that sign are emphasized in your personality and can become a theme through your life experiences. This theme can depend on the planet and sign in question.

Now it's time to get stuck into finding more about star signs. The following chapters will discuss the role that Astrology and the 12 zodiac signs can play in your life.

Chapter 1: The 12 Zodiac Signs

Everyone has always been in search of a deeper meaning to the reality that he or she lives in. Something that provides a reason for why we do what we do and who we are. Astrology is not a religion, but it can offer people a guideline for the interpretation of our present and our future. This information can show us the reasons behind disagreements or guide our steps forward in making a life-changing decision. Astrology indicates that nothing in life is chance. Everything happening at a time and place has a particular reason.

Babylonia is thought to be the birthplace of astrology. They used astrological charts to predict events. They then introduced their form of astrology to the Greeks in the early 4th century B.C. with such followers as Aristotle and Plato. It became regarded as a science and used by the Romans. In fact, the Romans established the zodiac names that we use today. The word "zodiac" came from the Greek term which means "circle of animals." The twelve lunar cycles and twelve constellations were linked to the seasons, and they were then assigned as identifiers (lion, scorpion, bull, etc.). Those twelve signs were then divided into four groups or "houses." Those houses are aligned with the elements of Air, Water, Fire, and Earth. These elements help to further our understanding of the positive and negative traits of our sign. This is based on Earth's daily rotation. At that time, only five planets were known, but it was believed that each of those planets represented a particular trait and area of life and possessed distinctive powers.

- Water signs: emotional and super-sensitive, highly intuitive and mysterious. These signs are Cancer, Pisces, and Scorpio.

- Fire signs: unpredictable, passionate, energetic, can get angry quickly but luckily, can forgive quickly, smart, creative, and idealistic. Come with loads of energy, they are strong and inspire others. These signs are Aries, Leo, and Sagittarius.

- Earth signs: realistic and conservative, but underneath, emotional. Connected to reality, practical, stable, and very loyal. These signs are Capricorn, Taurus, and Virgo.

- Air signs: thinkers, smart, communicative, analytical, and rational. Like giving people advice. Can sometimes be very superficial. These signs are Aquarius, Gemini, and Libra.

There are twelve (12) zodiac signs and each sign are represented by its own glyph, constellation, planet, gemstone, color, the day of the week, and more. Each sign has its own set of traits such as weaknesses, strengths and temperament. For centuries, people have been using this information to plot future choices, pick lovers, and to see what tomorrow will bring.

ARIES – March 20 through April 19			♈ Aries
Symbol:	The Ram	Quality	Cardinal
Day of the Week:	Tuesday	Ruling Planet:	Mars
Body Part:	head and face	Secret Desire:	To be number one
Gemstone:	Diamond	Color:	red
Best Compatibility – Overall:	Libra and Leo	Best Compatibility – Romantic:	Aquarius, Gemini, Leo, Sagittarius
What they like:	competitive games, new clothes, road trips, debating, expressing themselves with great verbal displays and through physical feats		

What they dislike:	losing, sharing their toys, being ignored, cramped spaces, the word "no"
Element:	Fire: One of 3 Fire Signs. Since it is the first Fire Sign, many Aries people are trailblazers and trendsetters. Known as "The Spark" – since the Cardinal quality is starting new things and a Fire Sign that spreads energy quite fast. Avoidant personality and always off to new things.
Ruling Planet:	Mars, a warrior planet with a masculine force representing aggression, instincts, and power, can be a source of life-force energy. The negative expression can show up as tactless, argumentative, insensitive, aggressive or confrontational. By being governed by Mars, Aries can be prone to anger but are also daring, highly energetic, impulsive, adventurous, and courageous. Since prone to anger, Aries can have a quick temper that is quick to explode.
Symbol:	The ram is based on the flying ram that provided the Golden Fleece in the mythological story of Jason and the Argonauts. In Greek mythology, Aries was associated with the Amon-Ra, who was depicted as a man with a ram's head. The word "aries" is also the Latin for ram. The glyph is to represent the curving horns of the ram which shows the determination and unceasing energy of this sign.

	Aries (cont.)
Personality & Outlook:	Aries have lots of energy and confidence. With their "can-do" attitude, they like new experiences and love to be number one. They can seem selfish or overly focused on themselves, and family and friends may have to remind them to share if their sense of entitlement gets out of control. They may seem abrasive, but will never back down from a challenge. Typically, Aries excel at anything involving competition and feels more alive when leading others and being in control. They can be impatient with those that are in a leadership position whom they feel are not their equal, because they do not like being told what to do by people who are less talented. Since Aries has lots of energy, they are great workers. Their motto can be "Live hard, love hard, work hard," but they can develop tunnel vision about a project which can sometimes make them seem self-centered. If an Aries doesn't get the pat on the back for their accomplishments, it can cause them to become rude and sarcastic. They dislike delays or inactivity. The presence of Aries typically marks the beginning of something stormy and high-energy.
Love/Relationship:	Aries need to take the initiative when it comes to romance. During the early stage of a romance, they will show their feelings before thinking things through completely. They may show their partner lots of attention and affection, even if what they receive is neutral/negative. Aries can be passionate and energetic and enjoys adventures. They may not have sufficient patience to focus on a partner as they have the need for excitement every day.

Money/Job:	A natural born leader, Aries likes issuing orders than receiving them. Their energy and quick mind usually mean that they walk one step ahead of everyone around them. When facing a challenge, they can quickly measure the situation and prepare a solution. They are not intimidated by competition. In fact, it encourages them to perform even better. Aries like to live in the present, so they tend not to focus on the future, which means they can sometimes make mistakes with regards to money decisions. But they will balance their earnings with what they have spent as they always seem to find a way to earn money.
Family/Friends:	Aries are typically tolerant and respectful to those who don't agree with their own. They will feel the most satisfied with a wide range of friends with different views. Honesty and directness are the best way to deal with an Aries.

	Aries (cont.)
Possible Descriptors:	pioneering, confident, dynamic, selfish, foolhardy, enthusiastic, confident, quick-witted, impatient, honest, adventurous, energetic, daredevil, courageous, quick-tempered, impulsive, courageous, determined, confident, passionate, optimistic, moody, impatient, aggressive
Famous Aries:	Lady Gaga, Celine Dion, Aretha Franklin, Keira Knightley, Victoria Beckham, Al Gore, Heath Ledger, Rosie O'Donnell, Gloria Steinheim, Emma Watson, Kourtney Kardashian, Pharrell Williams; Tommy Hilfiger, Maya Angelou, Robert Downey, Jr., Thomas Jefferson
Lucky Numbers:	1, 8, 17

TAURUS - April 20 through May 20

Taurus

Symbol:	The Bull	Quality	Fixed
Day of the Week:	Friday, Monday	Ruling Planet:	Venus
Body Part:	neck, throat, jaw	Secret Desire:	To own the best of everything
Gemstone:	Emerald	Color:	green, pink
Best Compatibility – Overall:	Scorpio, Cancer	Best Compatibility – Romantic:	Cancer, Virgo, Capricorn, Pisces
What they like:	cooking, photography, gardening, mountains, great music, satin sheets, gourmet food, high-quality clothes, working with hands		
What they dislike:	being rushed, wasting money, dirty things, hotels, mornings, sudden changes, complications, insecurity, synthetic fabrics		
Element:	Earth: known as "The Stone," it relies on its Fixed quality of stability and the Earth element stay consistent. Some may see them as stubborn.		
Ruling Planet:	Venus is the planet of love, luxury and beauty, pleasure, romance, love, femininity, and art		
Symbol:	The glyph depicts the head of the bull with horns. The bull shows the stubbornness, security, and slow/stead habits of this sign.		

Personality & Outlook:	They are typically grounded, unless a hot-button issue has them passionate and heated up. Taurus loves the arts, luxury, and nature. Since Taurus is an Earth Sign, they enjoy nature, but since they like luxury, they will not be roughing it. As they like luxury, they can sometimes be seen as materialistic. Relaxed and peaceful, they are slow to anger, but once engaged, it can be explosive. Taurus enjoys sensual pleasures but look for stability in their lives. Not in a hurry, Taurus is slow to make decisions and may take a long time to commit. But once they do commit, they take it seriously. The way for them to learn is through experience. A Taurus will almost always finish what they have started; usually making a well-informed, correct decision. However, they can be stubborn, which means they might be difficult to get along with, especially in a group project if they are not the leader. Can sometimes be unable to let feelings go. The chief qualities of a Taurus are perseverance and patience.

Taurus (cont.):

Love/Relationship:	Taurus is the Zodiac's most possessive sign. Male Taurus tends to marry for life and remain dedicated companions, parents, and lovers. Female Taurus is fully committed to a relationship and will be stubborn and slow to leave. But, when/if they feel acutely unappreciated for long enough, they will leave.
Money/Job:	Taurus loves money and will work hard to earn it. As they are reliable, hardworking, patient, and thorough, they will stick firmly to what they are working on. Stability is the key. The materials, pleasures, and rewards they earn can provide their sense of value. Their finances are typically organized and paid on time, saving is part of the plan. As they make money easily, they are suited in careers such as banking, economists, financial advisors, political leaders, art, cooking, and agriculture.
Family/Friends:	Taurus is loyal and always willing to lend a hand. However, they must build trust before any friendship can deepen. Some maintain friendships from childhood their entire life. Once they have established a connection, they will do whatever is necessary to nurture the relationship. Home and family are very important, and they love kids and respects family routines. Taurus loves to laugh and spend time with family and will enjoy hosting house parties and cooking for a room full of people. Taurus collects things, invisible and visible, and sometimes even people. This Earth Sign is known to hold resentment for a long time.
Possible Descriptors:	reliable, possessive, loving, patient, inflexible, persistent, determined, resentful, placid, warm-hearted, self-indulgent, greedy, materialistic, stubborn, stable, conservative, disciplined, loyal, honest, dependable, strong-willed, grounded, realistic

Famous Taurus:	Adele, Al Pacino, David Beckham, Stevie Wonder, Cher, Chris Brown, Channing Tatum, Dwayne Johnson, Megan Fox, George Clooney, Tina Fey, William Shakespeare, James Monroe, Ulysses Grant, Harry Truman
Lucky Numbers:	2, 6, 9, 12, 24

GEMINI – May 21 through June 20

Gemini

Symbol:	Twins	Quality	Mutable
Day of the Week:	Wednesday	Ruling Planet:	Mercury
Body Part:	shoulders, arms, hands	Secret Desire:	To have all the answers.
Gemstone:	pearl or moonstone	Color:	light-green, yellow
Best Compatibility – Overall:	Sagittarius, Aquarius	Best Compatibility – Romantic:	Aries, Leo, Libra, Aquarius, Sagittarius
What they like:	comedy clubs, cell phones, guitars, fast cars, books, obscure music, trendy clothes		
What they dislike:	Small-minded people, repetition, being confined, dress codes, being alone, silence, authority figures, routines, and nature.		
Element:	Air (first air element of the zodiac). Gemini exhibits great creative synergy, connecting people to each other. Air Sign which can sometimes be known as "The Cool Breeze." Embodying the Mutable quality inherent in a refreshing shift of consciousness, this kind of insight is indicative of the Air element. Although, some believe people that this Air Sign is "all flash and no substance." Air element – all aspects of the mind are connected.		
Quality:	Mutable: As a mutable sign, they know that all things must change, and they are prepared for that eventuality. They can adapt to change rather easily since they are comfortable with it. A plan can be brought to life by a Cardinal sign, then built by a fixed sign, and then polished and perfected by a mutable sign.		
Ruling Planet:	Mercury: represents intellect, logic, perception, thinking, and communication. Mercury represents communication, movement, and writing. With the connection to Mercury, Geminis are great		

	communicators, debaters, and intellectuals. Because they are intellectual and multi-taskers, they find it hard to focus on a task for longer periods of time.
Symbol:	Twins or the Roman numeral II is used as a representation to show the duality of this Sign. The twins also show creativity, communication, and resourcefulness which are vital to this Air Sign.

Personality & Outlook	As Gemini is ruled by the dual sign of twins, their energy circulates in a frenzied, quick way. They enjoy witty wordplay and dynamic dialogue, an intellectual meeting of the mind, and a kindred spirit. With a fondness for chatting, they may develop a weakness for gossip and embellishment. Gemini can inspire a roller-coaster ride. They like fast cars, funky new gadgets, trend-setting clothes, games and puzzles; and may seem like they have multiple personalities. Rarely do they like to do anything all alone. Communication is a key element, so they are great at parties, because they can find almost anything to talk about. Led by curiosity, they are adventurous by nature and engage in travel as often as they can afford. People are drawn to them because of their airy and light sparkle. Geminis will crave intellectual stimulation and will push themselves mentally, physically, and spiritually. This means that they end up knowing a little bit about a lot of things. But, they can also be sharp-tongued, selfish, and inconsiderate, thinking only of their own wants. They can also be very superficial with their knowledge, displaying it only for show. They love vibrant colors. Generally optimistic, they despise boredom and have a great sense of humor. A Gemini will enjoy being the center of attention. If they perceive a situation does not seem to be in their favor, they will leave it (career, marriage, relationship, friendship). Male Gemini will change jobs often, while females will leave relationships because they are bored. They can have a tendency to suddenly get serious, thoughtful or restless. Since it is represented by twins, some Gemini feels as if their other half is missing. This leads them to seek new friends, mentors,

	colleagues, loves, and other people to interact with.
Love/Relationship:	May date and flirt a lot before they find a match for their intellect and energy. Since they need passion, variety, and excitement, when they pick, it will be a person who combines lover, friend, and someone to talk to. Geminis will be faithful and determined to treasure their love interest. Some important aspects of the relationship will be excitement, communication, physical contact, and passion. The biggest challenge for a Gemini is to find an emotion and relationship that lasts and avoid any superficial bond that can be disappointing. They have a different perspective on life, one of movement, but are rarely certain of their own direction.

	Gemini (cont.)
Money/Job:	Any suitable job must challenge their minds. Geminis make excellent writers, artists, inventors, journalists, designers, speakers, traders, lawyers, orators, entrepreneurs, or preachers. Inventive, skillful, and smart, they have the need for a dynamic working environment that can provide lots of social contacts. It is important that the workplace not keep them trapped in a routine. Most Geminis do not focus on where the money comes from or how to earn it.
Family/Friends:	Geminis love to spend time with family and friends, especially the younger members. As they love to chat, they will have an abundance of social contacts. In order to stay engaged with family/friends, they will need to be communicated with regularly. The family is very important to a Gemini. The responsibilities of maintaining a family may be a challenge for them, but they are great at multi-tasking, so will use these skills as a parent.
Possible Descriptors:	versatile, youthful, adaptable, nervous, tense, communicative, witty, smart, superficial, inconsistent, eloquent, chatty, lively, cunning, inquisitive, anxious, fascinating, original, charming, resourceful, wise, and adventurous, selfish, sharp-tongued, inconsiderate
Famous Gemini:	Angelina Jolie, Kanye West, Prince, Johnny Depp, Donald Trump, Tupac Shakur, Macklemore, Kendrick Lamar, Iggy Azalea, Blake Shelton, Kate Upton, Amy Schumer, John F. Kennedy, George Bush, Harriet Beecher Stowe, George Orwell,
Lucky Numbers:	5, 7, 14, 23

CANCER – June 21 through July 22

Symbol:	Crab	**Quality**	Cardinal
Day of the Week:	Monday, Thursday	**Ruling Planet:**	Moon
Body Part:	Stomach, chest	**Secret Desire:**	To take care of friends and family
Gemstone:	Ruby	**Color:**	white
Best Compatibility – Overall:	Capricorn, Taurus	**Best Compatibility – Romantic:**	Taurus, Virgo, Pisces, Capricorn
What they like:	working with kids, gourmet meals, helping loved ones, relaxing near or in water, museum/art galleries, intramural sports, home-based hobbies, hosting parties.		
What they dislike:	playing with art supplies, tacky clothes, puttering in the kitchen, being rushed, paying full price, shopping for antiques, listening to live music, public speaking, frozen dinners.		
Element:	Water sign sometimes known as "The Rain." The first water sign, Cancer is a fluid sign that gets the creativity and emotions flowing. This makes those under this Water Sign excellent caretaker, as they frequently make sure everyone around them is contented and happy. This can give them a deep need to spend time with family. As a water sign, it means they have a deep and mysterious side.		
Quality:	Cardinal signs are characterized by starting things. They are visionaries and trailblazers. They may get lost during their journey, but what they find along the way will change things for the better. But, once they start something new, they may not stay around long enough to see it finished.		
Ruling Planet:	Moon: represents moods, the feminine, emotions, intuition, mothers, and children. It affects our moods		

	more than any other planet. Rules the inner self, bringing to life the deepest desires of the soul and cravings of our emotions. Since the Moon governs Cancer, they tend to be curious about habits and traditions, and they can be changeable and adaptive. However, they also need a lot of reassurance, can be demanding and are very timid.
Symbol:	The glyph represents either a crab with sideways claws or a woman's breasts, as this sign represents mothers and women. This shows the nurturing, feminine qualities of this Water Sign, and that Cancer is the caretaker of the zodiac rooting for the family, children, and home.

	Cancer (cont.)
Personality & Outlook:	Cancer will cling to a job for security and beloved family members/pets. It is important for them to set up a cozy and safe space. For them, change can be threatening. The essence of the energy of Cancer is sensitivity, feminity, domesticity, maternal instincts, compassion, romance, caretaking, and creativity. The negative energy of a Cancer leans to gossip, being hypersensitive, cliques, and being overly competitive. Their intuitions and emotions can overshadow logic and intellect. They are guided by their emotion and heart. Since they are guided by the moon, they may have emotional patterns that are beyond their control. They may play it too safe and can end up feeling smothered, which can then devolve into co-dependence or coddling. Cancers are homebodies at heart, especially female ones, and can be passionate foodies who love to eat and cook. As homebodies, they love house parties and are great with pets and kids, so they make excellent parents and caretakers. They may sometimes make a step like a crab – sideways – in order to face a fight or obtain a goal. They tend to grasp onto what makes them happy and refuse let go. Those under the sign of Cancer need to be needed and want to know they matter. And if their needs are not met, they may turn moody, shy, reserved, clingy, insecure, or brooding. They also have an offbeat sense of humor. They are good listeners, dependable and reliable. They are deeply intuitive and sentimental and can be challenging to get to know.
Love/Relationship:	The thing that is most important for them are their feelings, as emotions are very important to Cancer. They wear their heart on their sleeves

	and are gentle and caring. They prefer a person who can understand them, even when they are not talking. Their affection for anyone who is flaky, superficial or unreliable will be fleeting. They enjoy being in a committed relationship so they can have a sense of security. They may change their beliefs and opinions to match those that they love because that love is important. When in a relationship with Cancer, never take for granted any understanding, love or compassion they show you.
Money/Job:	A Cancer will roll up their sleeves to get the job done and get it done right. Typically, they work better alone than in a group. Loyal to their employers. Good career choices: gardener, nurse, housekeeper, decorator, politician.

	Cancer (cont.)
Family/Friends:	Since a Cancer is dedicated to their family, they can make unhealthy choices just to keep a healthy image of a family in place. This could lead them to choosing partners who repeat a cycle of abuse or bad behavior. Cancers communicate easily. Since this is a Sign of family, they enjoy having fun at the comfort of their homes in a more familiar atmosphere and will diligently preserve family memories. They are intuitive and compassionate. When they are content with their personal lives, they can be a parent that is very caring and has deep bond with their children.
Possible Descriptors:	loving, moody, emotional, imaginative, touchy, clingy, sensitive, intuitive, shrewd, cautious, protective, sympathetic, compassionate, romantic, maternal, hypersensitive, co-dependent, shy, reserved, insecure, brooding, sentimental
Famous Cancers:	Meryl Streep, Tom Cruise, Ariana Grande, Selena Gomez, Khloe Kardashian, Kourtney Kardashian, Vin Diesel, Robin Williams, Lindsay Lohan, Courtney Love, Pamela Anderson, O.J. Simpson, Gerald Ford, George W. Bush, Nathaniel Hawthorn, Ernest Hemingway, Emily Bronte, Vera Wang,
Lucky Numbers:	2, 3, 15, 20

LEO – July 23 through August 23

Symbol:	lion	Quality	Fixed
Day of the Week:	Sunday	Ruling Planet:	Sun
Body Part:	heart, upper back, spine	Secret Desire:	To rule the world.
Gemstone:	Peridot	Color:	gold, yellow-orange
Best Compatibility – Overall:	Aquarius, Gemini	Best Compatibility – Romantic:	Aries, Gemini, Libra, Sagittarius
What they like:	bright colors, theater, fun with friends, expensive things, being admired, holidays		
What they dislike:	being ignored, not being treated as an important person, facing difficult reality		
Element:	Fire sign sometimes known as "The Bonfire." Fire combined with the fixed nature edifies all around those and provides warmth. The second fire sign of the zodiac, Leo turns up the heat and are typically natural born leaders and magnetic performers.		
Quality:	Fixed sign; able to take the imaginative idea from a Cardinal sign and bring it to life into something real. Leo is trustworthy individuals who like a clear and concrete "to do" list.		
Ruling Planet:	Sun: representing life, vitality, ego, creativity, and expression. Typically, the sun constitutes a masculine ego and the life force.		
Symbol:	The glyph depicts a lion with a mane and both sides of a heart. A lion represents boldness, passion, drama, and playful qualities of this sign.		
Personality & Outlook:	Leos are in charge, regal, and proud. They like relaxation, comfort, and warmth. Leo will focus on the big picture, not the small details or fine print. Typically, they will have no patience for boring, complicated, or overly-involved. As natural leaders, they don't do well when they have to take orders. Love is most important		

to Leos. To be loved and have someone to love is their primary motivation. Their feelings will be hurt if they go unrecognized for an accomplishment. People will be drawn to them because of their warmth and energy. Leos tend to be honest, decent, and do the right thing. Appreciate luxury, materials goods, and organization but have a weakness for extravagance. With a great sense of self-worth, they can sometimes cross over into arrogance. They may end up smothering their mates and friends, which may cause some people to leave them. They will find this devastating, since Leo is all about family and community. Since they are generous and loyal, Leos will have a lot of friends. With self-confidence, they are good at leading a group toward a common goal. In love with life and warmhearted with a healthy sense of humor, Leos are good at taking the initiative necessary to resolve complicated situations. They are comfortable with asking for what they

Leo (cont.)

Personality & Outlook (cont.)	need, but can unconsciously neglect what those around them need because they are in their own pursuits and search for self-awareness. Leos love attention and must have it at all costs. They can be materialistic and high maintenance.
Love/Relationship:	Sincere and passionate, Leos demonstrate their feelings with ease. They are loyal, fun, respectful, and generous. Will typically take on the role of the leader in any relationship. But this may end up being aggravating to their partner if they impose their will too frequently and with a heavy hand. A Leo needs a partner who is reasonable, self-aware, reasonable, and can match their level of intelligence.
Money/Job:	Highly energetic, ambitious, and creative, Leos like to be busy. Once they are dedicated to a job or career, they will work hard and do it just right. The best position is for them to hold is for them to be their own bosses or manage others with little supervision. Leos like jobs that allow them to express artistic talent. Like to be surrounded by cutting-edge gadgets and money comes easily to them, but they spend it less responsibly. Generous at heart, they may end up getting taken advantage of by friend or acquaintance by giving out money. They can excel and use their talents to shine like their governing Sun in the entertainment field.
Family/Friends:	They are a loyal friend, generous, and faithful. Leos are born with the need to help others and are good at doing so since they are strong and reliable. They do not like to be alone, since they seem to get their self-esteem from their interactions with family and friends. They are tuned into their feelings, emotions, and mindset more than others. Family may not be their first

	priority but will do whatever they can to protect their loved ones.
Possible Descriptors:	generous, faithful, loving, bossy, dogmatic, expansive, creative, interfering, pompous, patronizing, warm-hearted, enthusiastic, broad-minded, regal, proud, honest, arrogant, passionate, energetic, intelligent
Famous Leo:	Mila Kunis, Madonna, Daniel Radcliffe, Chris Hemsworth, Halle Berry, Charlize Theron, J.K. Rowling, Robert DeNiro, Anna Kendrick, Tom Brady, Arnold Schwarzenegger, Whitney Houston, Jennifer Lawrence, Bill Clinton, Coco Chanel, Jennifer Lopez, Barack Obama
Lucky Numbers:	1, 3, 10, 19

VIRGO August 23 through September 23

Symbol:	Maiden	Quality	Mutable
Day of the Week:	Wednesday	Ruling Planet:	Mercury
Body Part:	stomach, waist, digestive system	Secret Desire:	To be a hero
Gemstone:	Sapphire	Color:	grey, beige, pale yellow
Best Compatibility – Overall:	Pisces, Cancer	Best Compatibility – Romantic:	Taurus, Cancer, Scorpio, Capricorn, Pisces
What they like:	long showers with deeply scented soaps, outdoor concerts, laptops, magazines, trivia games, childhood friends		
What they dislike:	spicy food, vulgar people, laziness, leaving home		
Element:	This Earth sign is sometimes known as "The Landslide." They make an impact in the material world. As the second Earth sign, Virgo builds a plan around the foundation that Taurus put in place. Virgo's energy motivates us to try new ways to do old projects. This energy can also get people stuck in "what if" mode and make them anxious or nervous.		
Quality:	Mutable sign: Virgos know that all things must change and must prepare everyone for that eventuality. They can adapt to new conditions since they are comfortable with change.		
Ruling Planet:	Mercury: representing intellect, logic, perception, thinking and communication, the ability to multi-task and check off the never-ended activity list. Roman god Mercury, the winged messenger, who carried out the tasks of the gods.		
Symbol:	The glyph is designed to depict either a maiden carrying a shaft of wheat, intestines or virginity. The		

	use of the maiden shows the qualities of innocence and serving for this sign.
Personality & Outlook:	Virgos are usually cool, calm, and mild-mannered on the surface, but underneath there is lots of activity. They are usually thinking, calculating, and assessing the situation. Gardening is one of their favorite hobbies, since they are very nurturing and love to grow things. This is perfect for them as they enjoy alone time as well. Since they tend to be detail-oriented, Virgos make excellent strategists. However, they can get overburdened because they struggle to say "no" to those asking for help. This can also cause them to be taken advantage by those that are aware of this. Kind, good-natured, patient, they love to laugh and can be sympathetic listeners. Male Virgos are very committed to a relation, almost never walking away from it, unless they are betrayed.

	Virgo (cont.)
Personality & Outlook (cont.):	Female Virgos are very good at parenting, being dedicated mothers, and may even mother kids that aren't theirs. This includes playing nursemaid as they are very aware of health matters (however, this can sometimes lead them to be hypochondriacs). But, they can also be critical or judgmental about anyone they feel is not living up to their potential. They are very opinionated, and they will express that opinion even to those that didn't ask to hear it. Although careful, they can also be a little blunt in delivering their message which may come across a little sharp. Although they pay attention, they worry that they might miss a detail that will change a situation they cannot remedy. This can cause them to get stuck in a loop that can make them critical of themselves and others. This may also cause them to become a perfectionist. In this regard, they love organization, order, cleanliness, and dedication. They also have a well-developed sense of speech and writing (communication). However, Virgos can be shy and only open up to people they trust. They are also very sensual when they open up in love and romance.
Love/Relationship:	Virgos need to feel safe before they expose themselves and be vulnerable. They will pursue a potential partner so the romance can provide the love and self-worth they lack. A stable, long-term relationship is preferred over multiple one-night stands. Trust needs to be built slowly and patiently, and they should be nurtured and cared for. Virgos are attracted to intelligence.
Money/Job:	Their approach allows them to excel at a number of careers, especially those requiring organization skills, paperwork, and problem-solving. Virgos are hard-working, practical, and analytical. They have

| | a great eye for details and are very attuned to matters of health. They are very good in service industry and excel in jobs including: nurses, critics, doctors, writers, journalists, teachers, typists, caregivers, counselors, and psychologists. Typically, Virgos are very good at saving money and will put something away for a rainy day. Their preference is for a practical and economical solution. However, sometimes this can come across as cheap and stingy. |

	Virgo (cont.)
Family/Friends:	They know how to solve problems and this makes them a good person to go to for advice. Virgos will nurture the family and friends that surround them. To become closer and more intimate with a Virgo, do something good for someone you know or your community. Good deeds are a way to their inner circle. Tradition is important, and they are very proud of their heritage and ancestry and dedicated to their family. Will be especially attentive to elderly and sick grandparents, aunts, uncles, and other family members.
Possible Descriptors:	diligent, intelligent, cool, patient, modest, overcritical, fussy, meticulous, practical, analytical, shy, reliable, worrier, harsh, perfectionist, conservative, calm, calculating, kind, critical, judgmental
Famous Virgos:	Beyoncé, Michael Jackson, Bernie Sanders, Cameron Diaz, Paul Walker, Kobe Bryant, Jimmy Fallon, Flo Rida, Adam Sandler, Pink, Sean Connery, Amy Poehler, Lyndon B. Johnson, Mary Shelley, Leo Tolstoy, Agatha Christie, Stephen King
Lucky Numbers:	5, 14, 15, 23, 32

LIBRA September 23 through October 23

Libra

Symbol:	Scales	Quality	Cardinal
Day of the Week:	Friday	Ruling Planet:	Venus
Body Part:	lower back, butt	Secret Desire:	To be loved and love in return
Gemstone:	Opal	Color:	pink, green
Best Compatibility – Overall:	Aries, Sagittarius	Best Compatibility – Romantic:	Aquarius, Gemini, Leo, Sagittarius
What they like:	harmony, gentleness, sharing with others, the outdoors (outdoor concerts prime), poetry, good books, lively debates, expensive jewelry, rich food, designer clothes		
What they dislike:	violence, injustice, loudmouths, conformity, unhappy people, dull people, practical people, bullies, pressure to make a decision and hearing "maybe".		
Element:	Cardinal Air sign sometimes known as "Exhaling," Libras put new energy out into the world. Some may see people with this sign as "all talk and no action." However, as the second air sign, it builds on Gemini's expansive gusts of air, and Libra then shapes them into winds of grace, good manners, and charm. This means, you may change without even knowing you are doing so. Libra inspires a successful relationship through compromise which may include inspiring teamwork.		
Quality:	Cardinal sign: Libra begins the Fall season so it is considered a leader and is typically "idea" people. Those under this sign are trendsetters and prize originality and like to be first.		
Ruling Planet:	Venus: The planet represents femininity, pleasure, romance, love, luxury, beauty and art. Venus, the goddess of love, adds charm and enhances everything she touches such as beauty, your personality, fashion, food, art, etc.		

Symbol:	This is the only sign that is represented by an object, not a living thing. The glyph represents the scales, symbolizing harmony and balance. This is displayed by the fairness and equality of those under this sign.
Personality & Outlook:	Libras need to remain aware and keep balance in family, work, recreational, health, and spirit. As they need to weigh all the options before making a decision, they can seem indecisive. What makes them unhappy is to see those around them unhappy, since they do not like to see others unhappy. Peace and harmony are the keys to happiness for a Libra. However, they do have such a strong sense of fair play

	Libra (cont.)
Personality & Outlook (cont.)	that if they think they (or others) are being treated unfairly, this may lead to conflict. A person under this sign might benefit from practicing meditation, in order to provide balance in their life, but most will at least enjoy some type of physical exercise that involves a mental component. They don't necessarily like to be the leader, but do want to ensure that their voices are heard. Although they like justice, equality and balance, they can carry a grudge. They will try to avoid confrontations but hate being alone, the partnership is important to them. Possess a strong intellect and a keen mind. Tend to be fond of expensive, material things and will dress well. Kind and considerate, romance, love, and marriage are a must for Libra. They are perhaps the most popular of the signs of the Zodiac and make the best friends.

Love/Relationship:	Finding a life partner will probably be one of the main priorities in Libra's life, and they should pick someone who encourages the expression of their own opinions. For a truly happy relationship, their partner should enhance the partnership with travel, music, art, and expensive gifts. Libra may be best satisfied by a partner who can set clear boundaries, thereby protecting them but without endangering their pride. Once they have that romantic relationship, the primary goal will be to maintain peace and harmony. Libra is the sign of marriage, so most people under this sign will go the traditional route. Even though they are flexible as an Air Sign, they will still gravitate to tradition and their journey will eventually lead to an officiant and bouquet. Part of the inspiration for this may be to create a certain image for the outer world. Since Libra is connected to Scorpio, they are sexual and seek a meaningful relationship where a complete surrender of body and soul can occur. Libra corresponds to the Seventh House (the Marriage House) which deals with the law, marriage and divorce, partnerships, and alliances. No other sign of the Zodiac requires romance and marriage like the Libra.

	Libra (cont.)
Money/Job:	Whatever career path they seek, Libras will not typically become a workaholic as they are more focused on the balance in their life. Balancing family, private time, work, and spouse is the key to their happy life. They will be loved if they become a leader, but do not necessarily have a penchant for this as they struggle with decision making and may lack the initiative to organize their employees. If they do rise to a position of power, they will work very hard to deserve those privileges that go with the position. Since they search for equality, truth and justice, they are good judicial officers, lawyers, diplomats and their artistic side can make them good composers or designers. The money is usually under control, but that may be a fluke because they can't decide what to indulge their finances in. They do like expensive material things. But rarely do they left their spending get the better of them and only occasionally indulge in fine clothes or expensive jewelry.

Family/Friends:	Highly social, Libras put their friends in the limelight, but can sometimes choose friends that allow them to feel superior. Their friends may struggle with their indecisive nature when planning activities. But, if they are not the initiator of the friendship, they will participate whole-heartedly. Since they are tactful and can remain calm, they often mediate between themselves and others and also between other friends who are in conflict. Libras can be self-sacrificing for the good of the family, but will also use guilt as a weapon against them. May agree with stronger family members simply to keep peace and harmony in the house. They may embrace parenting as a way to share their knowledge and views, but only if they are secure with their own inner sense of power.
Possible Descriptors:	Charming, cooperative, diplomatic, gracious, fair-minded, social, indecisive, peaceful, fair, tactful, honest, open-minded, deceitful/lying, vain, frivolous, superficial, vacillating, conservative, refined, tactful, honest, open-minded, loyal, faithful, sociable, urbane, idealistic, diplomatic, indecisive
Famous Libra:	Bruno Mars, Scott Fitzgerald, John Lennon, Simon Cowell, Snoop Dogg, Eminem, F. Ralph Lauren, Kim Kardashian, Zac Efron, Gwen Stefani, Mahatma Gandhi, Vladimir Putin, Jimmy Carter, Dwight D. Eisenhower, Donna Karan
Lucky Numbers:	4, 6, 13, 15, 24

SCORPIO-October 23 through November 22

Symbol:	Scorpion	Quality	Fixed
Day of the Week:	Tuesday	Ruling Planet:	Pluto
Body Part:	crotch, reproductive organs	Secret Desire:	To have complete and total control
Gemstone:	Topaz or citrine	Color:	scarlet, red, rust
Best Compatibility – Overall:	Taurus, Cancer	Best Compatibility – Romantic:	Cancer, Virgo, Capricorn, Pisces
What they like:	truth, facts, being right, teasing, longtime friends, spicy food, danger, probing questions, underground music, unique items, organic food		
What they dislike:	revealing secrets, dishonesty, passive people, simple-minded people, personal questions, insincere flattery, living at someone else's house		
Element:	Fixed Water Sign, which can be called "Ice." The Cancer's tides are directed by the second water sign into forceful torrents of energy. It is connected more closely to the darker side of life and the unexamined areas. This allows them to see beneath the surface into spirituality. They can sometimes be obsessed about a lover or project, displaying insecurity or jealousy.		
Quality:	Fixed sign Scorpio is a stabilizer, taking the creativity of Cardinal signs and starting to build the foundation of a plan. The Fixed quality shows the nature of the Water.		
Ruling Planet:	Pluto: the Underworld's Greek god and all things occult. Since Scorpio also has a lesser ruler in Mars (the Greek god of War) since Pluto was just found in the 1930s. Pluto represents power, healing, transformation, obsession, alchemy, and life and death (creation/destruction). Mars represents war, energy, anger, initiative, adventure, courage, and impulse.		

Symbol:	The glyph represents a scorpion with the pointy tail. Scorpion was used to represent intensity, depth, and obsessiveness.
Personality & Outlook:	Scorpios can crave time alone and will be annoyed if they don't get it. They are great secret keepers and feel their emotions more intensely than other signs, typically becoming self-aware at an earlier age. This makes emotions very important to a Scorpio. They believe in defending those that lack that ability and require being a leader. Scorpios are typically great leaders, since they are resourceful and alert to their surroundings. They excel at problem solving, and this leads them to also be interested in what makes people tick.

	Scorpio (cont.)
Personality & Outlook (cont.):	They will research topics and people until they find out the truth. They exert extreme self-control and those around them are expected to do so as well. Scorpio invented the word "vendetta," as they never forgive and forget and will definitely get even. Those under this sign also tend to be suspicious, pessimistic, stubborn, and occasionally even paranoid. However, they are also known for their calm and cool behavior. Scorpio love a good challenge, will thrive from it, and obstacles won't even dissuade them. They love winning.
Love/Relationship:	A sensual sign, intimacy and passion are very important to them. They desire to have honest and smart partners. Once a Scorpio falls in love, they are dedicated and faithful. They prefer to build a relationship slowly until they build trust and respect. Be careful when ending a relationship with a Scorpio and do your best to ensure that it is a mutual and amicable split, as this is the most vengeful sign in the zodiac. A Scorpio ex can be a very bad thing.
Money/Job:	Good at being a leader and management and when they set a goal for the team, company or themselves, they achieve it. The focus and determination they use in approaching a task make them good managers. However, they rarely mix business with friendship, so socializing at work will be at a minimum. Good jobs for a Scorpio are researcher, scientist, sailor, police, detective, physician, psychologist/counselor, and business manager. When it comes to money, they are disciplined enough to stick to a budget. Although they are not afraid of hard work to earn it, they are also not inclined to spend a lot of money.

Family/Friends:	Scorpios look for fairness and honesty when it comes to searching for a friend. Scorpios can make great friends, since they are dedicated and loyal. Smart and quick-witted, they prefer the company of fun-loving people who can keep up. However, if you let them down just once, there is probably no bouncing back from it. When they are hurt, they are very emotional, so it is hard to make them feel better. They are dedicated and they take good care of their family.

	Scorpio (cont.)
Possible Descriptors:	frank, determined, pessimistic, suspicious, courageous, stubborn and paranoid, honest, resourceful, brave, passionate, stubborn, constructive, distrusting, passionate, open, spiritual, affectionate, tender and loving, sensitive, obsessive, sincere, vengeful, persevering, strong-willed, intuitive, perceptive, jealous, secretive, violent, assertive, decisive
Famous Taurus:	Robert Louis Stevenson Sylvia Plath, Theodore Roosevelt, John Adams, Julia Roberts, Ryan Reynolds, Ryan Gosling, Emma Stone, Lorde, Calvin Kline, Puff Daddy, Kendall Jenner, Caitlyn Jenner, Kris Jenner, Bill Gates, Leonardo DiCaprio, Katy Perry, Drake, Hillary Clinton
Lucky Numbers:	8, 11, 18, 22

SAGITTARIUS - November 22 through December 22

Sagittarius

Symbol:	centaur or archer	Quality	Mutable
Day of the Week:	Thursday	Ruling Planet:	Jupiter
Body Part:	thighs, hips	Secret Desire:	To be the one to make the rules
Gemstone:	turquoise or tanzanite	Color:	blue
Best Compatibility – Overall:	Gemini, Aries	Best Compatibility – Romantic:	Aries, Libra, Leo, Aquarius
What they like:	freedom, traveling, being outside, philosophy, pets, flirting, laughing, karaoke, dares, books, stories that inspire		
What they dislike:	crazy theories, details, people who cling, being constrained, prejudice, boredom, being told "you can't," routine		
Element:	Fire Sign is sometimes known as "The Wildfire." The third and final Fire Sign, Sagittarius combines Aries' trailblazing with Leo's leadership to create an explosion of wisdom and action. Sagittarius pushes us to go after endless possibilities, as they are the eternal optimist.		
Quality:	Mutable: They know that all good things must change and their role is to help others prepare for the change. They will change to adapt to situations. Their mutable quality of unchecked energy shows up as a burst. However, that unchecked burst of energy may quickly burn out, just like a wildfire.		
Ruling Planet:	Jupiter: Represents luck, growth, abundance, expansion, higher learning, travel, and religion. Since the planet is the largest in the solar system, those under this sign can also have big		

	personalities. Jupiter was the most widely revered Roman god, leading Sagittarians to want the biggest and the best, sometimes to the point of over-indulgence.
Symbol:	The glyph represents the arrow of the centaur or an archer. The arrow of the glyph points upwards to show optimism and the higher spiritual ideal. This represents the honesty and wisdom of this sign.
Personality & Outlook:	Love discovering new things, travel, the open road, and meeting new people. Will be very unhappy tied to a normal routine, as they will become restless without variety. Highly intelligent, they enjoy learning and will question everything. Big daydreamers, but can get carried away with unrealistic or grandiose plans, and they sometimes lack in follow-through since they become easily sidetracked by new adventures. May focus on the big picture and get bogged down with details. With this daydreaming quality, they may come across as just a "big talker," promising more than they can deliver. But, with their generous, idealistic, and fun sense of humor, those around them will quickly forgive this shortcoming.
Sagittarius (cont.)	
Personality & Outlook (cont.):	Give them ample space, as they do not like being confined and will travel with an open mind. This penchant for spirituality and philosophy may inspire them to wander the world in search of the meaning of life. Sagittarius wants to constantly be in touch with the world in order to experience as much as possible. Freedom is priceless to them just so they can explore and travel. Honest and forthright, sometimes to the point of sometimes being tactless, they are open and very broad-minded.

Love/Relationship:	Considered to be the happiest of the signs. Willing to try almost anything, since they are incredibly playful, humorous, open, passionate, and expressive. It might take them a while to get serious and settle down, as they embrace diversity and change. This may cause them to go through a string of partners before finding the one they commit to. However, once truly in love, they are faithful, loyal, and completely dedicated. They do best with partners who are smart, sensitive and expressive.
Money/Job:	If they can envision their goal, they do almost anything to achieve it. They like a position with a changing atmosphere and different tasks. Good jobs: photographer, researcher, salesperson, artist, interviewers, reporter, talk-show host, travel agent, artist, ambassador, importer/exporter. Enjoy making/spending money. Doesn't much care where they will earn their money, but feel the need to take risks, even if they appear foolish or impractical. They typically believe that the universe will simply provide them with what they need. They are not good at managing the finances and money, as they are undisciplined and waste a lot of energy.
Family/Friends:	Usually surrounded by friends since they are fun to be with. They love to laugh and enjoy diversity in their circle of friends. Dedicated to family and generous with their time, affection, and help.
Possible Descriptors:	daydreamer, lucky, creative, generous, idealistic, impatient, tactless, curious, energetic, extroverted, enthusiastic, honest, tolerant, restless, outspoken, undisciplined, opportunistic, humorous, playful
Famous Sagittarius:	Brad Pitt, Taylor Swift, Miley Cyrus, Britney Spears, Sia, Winston Churchill, Mark Twain, Jay-Z, Frank Sinatra, Sammy Davis, Jr., Vanessa Hudgens, Scarlett Johannsson, Christina Aguilera, Jake Gyllenhaal, Chrissy Teigen, Emily Dickinson,

	Manolo Blahnik, Joseph Stalin
Lucky Numbers:	3, 7, 9, 12, 21

CAPRICORN December 22 through January 20

Capricorn

Symbol:	mountain goat	Quality	Cardinal
Day of the Week:	Saturday	Ruling Planet:	Saturn
Body Part:	skin, bones, knees, teeth	Secret Desire:	To have every need taken care of
Gemstone:	Garnet	Color:	brown, black
Best Compatibility – Overall:	Taurus, Cancer	Best Compatibility – Romantic:	Taurus, Virgo, Scorpio, Pisces
What they like:	music, family, quality craftsmanship, tradition, understated status, goals, titles, exclusive clubs, motorcycles, sports involving running, being in charge		
What they dislike:	a whole host of things at some point throughout their lives, careless mistakes, roaming without a plan, doing things without purpose, quitting, shouting in public		
Element:	Earth Sign sometimes called "The meteor" as they will go independently into new worlds. The Earth elements make Capricorn solid and absolute. The third and final Earth Sign, they combine the foundation of Taurus with Virgo's planning. Capricorns keep the big picture in view and are, therefore, good at strategy, and may inspire them to take on big goals.		
Quality:	Cardinal Sign, the first winter sign, which means they are lead or "idea" people. This means that they like originality and want to be a trendsetter (the first one to use/create something new).		
Ruling Planet:	Saturn: represents the structure, restrictions, time, authority, research, discipline, hard work, delay, obstacles, privation, pessimism, and lasting reward after a long struggle, and limitations. Saturn (aka Cronus) was Father Time. Saturn is the planet of repression, so Capricorn may hide a few freaky secrets under their calm exterior.		

Symbol:	The glyph represents the goat as a working-class animal and this sign is a working-class sign. Capricorn makes long-term plans, often earning awards and drawing acclaim. In some representations, the goat is combined with a fish's tail to show that imagination and creativity will work in combination with that planning.
Personality & Outlook:	Capricorn is usually goal-oriented and driven to succeed, so they will work hard and put in long hours. As achievement is very important, they tend to be self-disciplined and successful. Take life seriously and are not very tolerant of other people who do not. Very good at making decisions, since they are realistic and logical. Family-oriented, unless their family members are negative or harmful, in which case, they will ensure they keep distance between themselves and family. Dry sense of humor, sarcastic, so they may not be everyone's "cup of tea."

Capricorn (cont.)	
Personality & Outlook (cont.)	To those that don't know them well, they can seem dull or less imaginative since they are focused on the big picture. While on the surface they can come across as lacking in emotion, there is lots of activity running through their minds. May seem to be selfish or stingy and secretive with information, since they guard their hearts closely. Capricorns hate being wrong. Because their focus is on the material world, this can make them seem stiff and stubborn when it comes to changing their perspective when necessary. Can seem to be intolerant as they have a hard time accepting those that vary too much from their own perspective. Serious by nature and traditional, yet with an inner state of independence. Masters of self-control, those under this sign are very good at leading the way. They will learn from their mistakes, but they need to learn to forgive, so as to avoid being stuck in the past and alleviate their pessimistic nature. Capricorns can also be pessimistic and negative, especially if they perceive obstacles in their path.

Love/Relationship:	Although the beginning of a relationship with a Capricorn will be difficult, once you breach the outer defenses and they are in love, they will stay committed for a lifetime. For romance to be effective, it should be demonstrated through action, not just words. However, it still may take years before they open up enough to talk about their feelings. They may seem emotionally or lacking in compassion in dealing with their loved ones. Their partner will be able to rely on them as there will be a lasting bond between them that will accept the constant tendency to grow, change, and evolve. But any partner of Capricorn should not count on them compromising very often.

	Capricorn (cont.)
Money/Job:	Very career oriented. Will set very high standards for themselves. Their dedication, honesty, and perseverance will help them to achieve goals. Capricorns value hard work and loyalty the most, and this can offset negative traits of those they work with, even if that has less talent or intelligence. They don't mind putting in the extra hours, are resourceful, and will get the job done. Good with numbers and analysis. Best jobs would involve management, calculations, finance, politician, diplomat, mathematician, and possibly programming. They like tradition, so jobs that involve a lot of paperwork don't bother them (but the paperwork must be orderly and neat). Those under this sign value money and will be good at managing it and saving it. Can be good diplomats and politicians, as they are good at cutting through red tape and seeing the bottom line. Like all Earth signs, Capricorns have great savvy, acumen, and business skills, and are conservative with money and good with finances.
Family/Friends:	Although they are good friends and very loyal, Capricorns will not list a lot of people in their inner circle. Since they guard their hearts closely, it will take time for anyone new to get into their inner circle. They prefer to be around people who aren't nosy and don't ask too many questions. They are open-hearted and will choose friends who can carry on a lively, intelligent conversation, make them feel peaceful, and will be honest with them. Since they feel connected to everything in their past, friends can expect to hear the same stories told repeatedly, to look through old photos and watch family movies. As parents, they can be strict but are usually fair. Capricorns want to be respected for their role as head of the family.

Possible Descriptors:	Persevering, reliable, trustworthy, stable, persistent, patient, ambitious, self-reliant, logical, ambitious, good self-control, determined, diligent, honorable, miserly, sarcastic, pessimistic, unforgiving, realistic, grounded, careful, practical, loyal, prudent, humorous, disciplined, know-it-all, responsible, hard-working, down-to-earth, and charitable,

Capricorn (cont.)	
Famous Capricorn:	David Bowie, Muhammad Ali, Kate Middleton, Martin Luther King, Jr., Michelle Obama, Denzel Washington, Nicolas Cage, Meghan Trainor, Elvis Presley, Pitbull, Liam Hemsworth, Jared Leto, Howard Stern, Betty White, Richard Nixon, Nicolas Sparks, J.R.R. Tolkein, Edgar Allen Poe
Lucky Numbers:	4, 8, 13, 22

AQUARIUS January 20 through February 18

Aquarius

Symbol:	water bearer	Quality	Fixed
Day of the Week:	Saturday	Ruling Planet:	Uranus
Body Part:	ankles	Secret Desire:	To experience total freedom
Gemstone:	Amethyst	Color:	light blue or silver
Best Compatibility – Overall:	Leo, Sagittarius	Best Compatibility – Romantic:	Aries, Gemini, Libra, Sagittarius
What they like:	teaching, team sports, a cause/mission, computer programming, independent films		
What they dislike:	owing money, feeling isolated, injustice, drama queens		
Element:	An Air Sign sometimes referred to as "The Deep Breath." They instinctively know what thoughts are commonplace and will know what people want simply by being with them. Although, that does not necessarily make Aquarius one of them. The third and final Air Sign, it adds Gemini's gusts with the whirlwind that is Libra to create a gale of humanitarian causes. This makes them visionaries, causing them (and others) to get involved with a new cause, join a new social group, or have a mission in life. People born under a water sign see the world as a place full of possibilities.		
Quality:	Fixed sign – stabilizer who takes the creativity of the Cardinal and starts to build a plan.		

Ruling Planet:	Uranus: represents rebellion, revolution, emotional detachment, unpredictable energy, individualism, eccentricity, humanitarianism, fashion, modern science, and inventions. Uranus was the sky god. Some schools believe Aquarius is governed by dual planets: Uranus and Saturn. Saturn then adds privation, obstacles, delay, hard work, pessimism, and research to the mix. This combination makes Aquarians society's seekers, political agitators, and revolutionaries. The Saturn influence of pessimism can also put a lot of challenges in front of them. The ruling planet of Uranus has a timid, abrupt, and sometimes aggressive nature, but also a visionary quality. They can perceive the future, and they know their life plan for years to come.
Symbol:	The glyph represents water and the flow of energy or wavelength. One of the few signs not represented by an animal, but instead by an element. The waves of water express the humanitarianism of this sign.

	Aquarius (cont.)
Personality & Outlook:	Connection is at the core of this sign but on the surface, they may not seem very emotional. However, this is usually because Aquarius is preoccupied with helping others and exchanging ideas. Highly intelligent, energetic, and talented, they often crave time alone just to sit and think. Without the ability to do, they can become depressed. But in contrast, they dislike actually being lonely. This can also make them highly resentful if they believe their opinions are not valued. They can seem eccentric with their periods of intense self-reflection. You may see Aquarius running the gamut of emotional expressions from temperamental to uncompromising to aloof to lively. Deep thinkers, they are fascinated by gadgets and like to invent and tinker in the workshop. Without sufficient mental stimulation, they can become bored, and then they will lack motivation for a cause or project. Aquarius likes to fight for a cause, but can sometimes break promises to those involved. Although they have a reputation for being cold or distant, at least initially, they are actually generous with their time and resources. They just need to trust you before they express themselves. In searching for a cause, Aquarius can become too much of a dreamer, be unrealistic, or even impractical at times, losing touch with reality. Occasionally, even becoming fanatical in their views and destructive with their criticism.

Love/Relationship:	For those under this sign, intellectual stimulation is the best aphrodisiac. The best traits for a partner include good communication, imagination, openness, and a willingness to take risks. For a long-term relationship, integrity and honesty are the most essential traits. Once in love, they are totally committed, loyal, and will not be possessive.
Money/Job:	Career usually involves helping others as Aquarius are predominantly concerned with the welfare of others. They bring enthusiasm to whatever job they hold. Aquarius prefers a career that enables learning and development. Their intelligence, combined with a willingness to help out, inspires those around them. They are an unconventional type of visionary that likes to try to make humanity better. Careers that are a good fit: photography, pilot, teacher, writer, actor, but any situation where they can solve a problem without confines or guidelines may be enough to make any job desirable. Talented in balancing saving/spending money.

	Aquarius (cont.)
Family/Friends:	Very friendly and make friends everywhere they go. Great at networking. Friends and family of any Aquarius must have honesty and integrity, be creative and intelligent. Although they have a strong sense of duty to relatives, they will not maintain ties if those qualities are not met. Will do anything for a loved-one, including self-sacrifice. Aquarius corresponds to the Eleventh House (Friends House) which deals with social life, friendship, hopes, and wishes. Although Aquarius has a lot of friends, they also love to be by themselves, so a balance must be found. As they are very active and involved in social change, they will have a long list of people they know.
Possible Descriptors:	generous, patient, tolerant, friendly, unconventional, intelligent, energetic, talented, progressive, original, independent, aloof, philosophical, honest, humble, shy, driven, cautious, contrary, perverse, detached, eccentric, honest, forthright, reliable; tolerant, kind, considerate, helpful, withdrawn, , community-minded, humanitarian, impartial
Famous Aquarius:	Oprah Winfrey, Jennifer Aniston, Justin Timberlake, Alicia Keys, Bobby Brown, Sarah Palin, Michael Jordan, Ellen DeGeneres, Ed Sheeran, Shakira, John Travolta, Abraham Lincoln, Franklin Roosevelt, Ronald Reagan, Gertrude Stein, Charles Dickens, Christian Dior
Lucky Numbers:	4, 7, 11, 22, 29

PISCES-February 18 through March 20

Pisces

Symbol:	Fish	Quality	Mutable
Day of the Week:	Thursday	Ruling Planet:	Neptune
Body Part:	Feet	Secret Desire:	To find unconditional love.
Gemstone:	Aquamarine or Bloodstone	Color:	mauve, lilac, purple, violet, sea green
Best Compatibility – Overall:	Virgo, Taurus	Best Compatibility – Romantic:	Taurus, Cancer, Scorpio, Capricorn
What they like:	laughing, romance, long letters, dancing, walking on the beach, being alone, music, spiritual themes, romance, visual media, swimming, and games of chance		
What they dislike:	barking orders, daylight, bad designs, reality, noisy music, criticism, replaying the past, cruelty, and people who are a "know-it-all"		
Element:	A Water Sign sometimes referred to as "The Flood," since they reach everyone without a convention and leaves their mark on others long after an encounter. As the third and final water sign, it blends the sentimentality of Cancer with Scorpio's force, creating an ocean of emotions. Emotional expression of creativity plays a big role.		
Quality:	Mutable signs: They know things must change and are comfortable with change. As a mutable Water Sign, Pisces explores and adjusts themselves to the feelings of those around them. This Sign will often offer advice, information or sympathy, whichever is most appropriate.		

Ruling Planet:	Ruled by the planet Neptune: represents dreams, illusion, delusion, spirituality, theatrics, oneness, inspiration, deception, addictions. Neptune was the Greek god of the sea and renown for a furious temper. According to some, Pisces is ruled by dual planets, both Neptune and Jupiter. Jupiter deals with protection, expansiveness, generosity, opportunities, optimism, and luck.
Symbol:	Two fishes facing in opposite directions which show the duality of the Pisces nature. It can also show the plans lurking beneath the surface of this fantasy-oriented zodiac sign.
Personality & Outlook:	Pisces never like to see other people unhappy. Empathetic, they are driven to help those in need and can easily find themselves involved in someone else's drama. And by feeling things so deeply, this may lead them to become a constant worrier, which can then lead to indecision. Consequently, they may have a lack of follow-through because of an inability to make a decision. Can be serious daydreamers, but are generally very happy and vibrant. Pisces can be difficult to get to know, as they are frequently reticent to share things.
Pisces (cont.)	

Personality & Outlook (cont.):	Deeply religious, they can even sometimes be manic about their belief, which sometimes leads to bigotry or intolerance. Pisces generally don't like to hurt anyone's feelings and do not do well as leaders. Pisces are friendly, caring, intuitive, selfless, compassionate, and willing to help others. They may sometimes play the role of the victim or martyr in order to be the center of attention. Known to be one of the more tolerant signs, they are never judgmental and always forgiving. However, Pisces can be very secretive, deceptive, and calculating. As the final sign, some feel that this sign experiences the energy of all the other signs before it and are closest to the barrier between this world and the next. Can be very optimistic and love games of chance and can do well on stage dancing, singing, or acting; very big on participating or watching theater. Pisces can be easily discouraged and tend to give up easily in matters and can become very depressed due to their pessimistic outlook on life. Pisces can sometimes be easy to be persuaded, inspired, deceived, or convinced to buy something. Very impressionable, someone under this sign might give little or no resistance when they should. Consequently, they easily give in to temptation and lacks willpower.

Love/Relationship:	True romanticists, loyal, caring, gentle and unconditionally generous. Pisces are passionate lovers who want to feel a real connection. Short-term relationships are common. They can however, demonstrate jealousy on occasion. When it comes to love, Pisces' charisma plays a big part in their personality. Pisces has a sensitive nature and deep appreciation for the inner qualities of their lover. Those under this sign are the happiest when they are in a loving relationship or involved in a creative project. Pisces enjoys the romance, courting, dating, and everything in-between when beginning a relationship.

Pisces (cont.)

Money/Job:	Dedicated, Pisces will stay with one company for decades even if they are not completely happy there. They do the best in a career that allows them to use creative skill and to work with a charity. Good career choices include attorney, musician, social worker, veterinarian, salesperson, architect, or game designer. May work with charities or lost causes since they feel the need to make changes to the lives of others. Any non-profit would be lucky to have them as they are great problem-solvers, hard-working, dedicated, and reliable. They don't think much about money or making it, but see it as a means to achieving their goals. With spending habits, they can go down either path, either spending too much carelessly or spending nothing and being miserable.
Family/Friends:	Pisces can be the best friends you'll ever have, and they will put the needs of their friends and family members above their own needs. Loyal, devoted, compassionate, gentle and caring, your Pisces friend will try to resolve any problems as best they can. And don't think that you can hide it from them because they will intuitively sense if something is wrong. They are very expressive and will share their feelings with everyone around them, and they expect everyone they know to be as open as they are. Frequent and easy communication with friends and family is essential. Since they have an intuitive understanding of the life cycle, they achieve the best emotional relationships.

Possible Descriptors:	dreamy, deceptive, considerate, loving, affectionate, imaginative, intuitive, trustworthy, psychic, supportive, creative, artistic, broad-minded, tolerant, talented, secretive, calculating, creative, loyal, daydreamer, happy, vibrant, sympathetic, emotional, kind, earnest, idealistic, faithful , opportunistic, indolent, withdrawn
Famous Pisces:	Albert Einstein, Rihanna, Justin Bieber, Adam Levin, Carrie Underwood, Kesha, Steve Jobs, Kurt Cobain, Eva Longoria, Drew Barrymore, George Washington, Andrew Jackson, Victor Hugo, Dr. Seuss, Henrik Ibsen
Lucky Numbers:	3, 9, 12, 15, 18, 24

Chapter 2 Relationship Astrology:

Signs with the same element (Air, Water, Fire and Earth) can understand each other the best. However, there are complementary elements also: For example, Air blends well with Fire and Water blends with Earth. The strongest attraction usually lies with the opposing sign.

Here are each signs strongest compatibility:

Aries: Aquarius, Gemini, Leo, and Sagittarius

Aquarius: The combination of the vision of an Aquarius and the action of an Aries makes a very creative match. The relationship will not be dull as each can be quite competitive. They communicate really well. Both crave excitement and new experiences but understand the other's idealistic and enthusiastic outlook on life. The admiration between the two is mutual; Aries loves how unique Aquarius is, and Aquarius enjoys Aries energy. The connection is undeniable, but so are the differences as well. An Aries can think that their Aquarius partner can be too unpredictable and Aries can be too possessive. This making it crucial that both partners must keep reassuring the other that everything is secure and the relationship is important.

Gemini: Aries and Gemini have a connection on a physical and intellectual level. They are powerfully alike in which both are active and optimistic. These signs typically have great communication and thoroughly understand each other. Gemini values independence and will admire Aries's independent spirit. Arguments may arise if Aries becomes too controlling or takes Gemini's flirtatious nature too seriously. Together, they are well balanced. Aries want to do new things and Gemini wants to talk about them. Both signs have lots of energy, and Gemini's intelligence and ability to see all sides of a task will help Aries who loves to get started on projects full steam ahead. While

Gemini may waver on what projects to start, Aries is able to make the decision and can keep things on task. Both are ruled by Planets representing communication, but their approach may be different.

Leo: Sparks fly between an Aries and a Leo. Both Fire Signs are passionate, energetic, and competitive which means that there is a lot of action in this match. Since both Signs want to be in charge, this can create problems, but they have respect and admiration for each other. If they can simply take turns being in charge, they will have a more harmonious relationship. With fiery passion and a competition for domination, this match can be full of drama. Both proud and impatient, further drama can surface as Leo likes to have their ego stroked, but as this may bore Aries, they may not oblige. Leos are a flirt and may cause more drama. Despite these differences, Leo can be a great counselor for Aries. Both Aries and Leo are ruled by masculine energy planets, so they understand each other, since they come from the same place.

Sagittarius: These partners have much in common and are very compatible, being pioneers and explorers. They both crave adventure and new experiences, but this could be a match prone to accidents. Sagittarius may overlook little details, and Aries is always in a rush. But boredom may set in as both signs have energy to start new things, this could lead to never finishing anything. Aries and Sagittarius can make both great friends and terrific lovers. Since both are optimistic, problems are rare, but the need for independence can cause strife. Sagittarius has an even greater need for independence than Aries does. Although both signs are quick to forgive, Aries can be a bit more sensitive. Sagittarius occasionally speaks without thinking first and can spend some time apologizing for that.

Taurus: Pisces and Virgo

Pisces: Taurus and Pisces is a happy union. Taurus is practical while Pisces is idealistic. Both signs are nurturers and value stability and harmony. Pisces dreams and Taurus provides the grounding. Pisces offers kindness and gentle nature which Taurus appreciates in a lover. When Venus (Taurus' planet) and Neptune (Pisces planet) meet, a lovely spiritual bond is made. Both with feminine energy, together they epitomize an idealistic relationship, bordering on heavenly.

<u>Virgo</u>: A match between a Taurus and a Virgo is a practical match. Both Signs value practicality in every aspect of their daily lives. Sincere and devoted to each other, both have a lot of integrity. Taurus likes Virgo's quick mind while Virgo appreciates Taurus's strength. This relationship can take a while to develop since Virgo is cautious, but with the foundation, both are in it for the long-term. These two Signs value common sense and the practicality along with being materialistic. Virgo's tendency to analyze can lead to criticism and Taurus may take it too seriously. Virgo may be annoyed by Taurus's stubborn nature, which may cause Virgo to criticize more frequently. Neither should take the other too seriously.

Gemini: Aquarius, Gemini and Libra

<u>Aquarius</u>: This pair can create quite a stimulating mental connection; Aquarius is full of ideas and Geminis love that. Both will need their independence; but since it is mutual, they will both understand this requirement. Aquarius may sometimes feel that Gemini drags their feet a little too much and Gemini may feel that Aquarius is a little too stubborn. But neither of these should manifest as major problems. In general, they understand each other and mesh well. Both have a great deal of energy and their minds are quick, sharing new and better ideas. With Aquarius' willpower, they will be more likely to put their ideas into action. Both Signs just hate wasting time, and Aquarius will help Gemini to focus but must be careful to give Gemini plenty of space and freedom, as a Gemini doesn't like to feel pushed into anything.

<u>Gemini</u>: Two Geminis are really like four people forming a bond, and will never be boring. Both will have the same need for

intellectual stimulation, and will almost always be talking, but it will work by a constant exchange of ideas. Two Geminis together will be all about freedom and communication and may end up being the most favorite couple in their circle of friends. Avoiding competition and cooperating will ensure the relationship goes more smoothly and remain happy.

Libra: A personality of two halves loves the balance that Libra has. And Libra will be interested in the talkative, smart aspects of Gemini. While Gemini focuses on ideas, Libra loves beauty and art. So, a trip to an art museum and then coffee afterward to discuss would be their perfect afternoon. Both have a lot of mental energy and can brainstorm all sorts of great ideas when they come together. Luckily, Libra also has the initiative to put ideas into action, which is something the Gemini may be lacking in.

Cancer: Pisces and Scorpio

Pisces: Both Cancer and Pisces are sympathetic and tolerant. Pisces can get energized by Cancer's ideas. Cancer can guide Pisces with their practical nature and Pisces can show Cancer a world of spirituality and creativity. While Pisces will have a minimal amount of 'stuff', Cancer loves possessions, desiring comfort and luxury. This may seem as they would be at an un-match, but the emotional depth shared by Cancer and Pisces can make it a highly rewarding match.

Scorpio: Both intense energy Signs can combine well with each partner's strengths balancing the weaknesses of the other. A relationship between these two will usually be heightened by a strong sexual attraction. Cancer and Scorpio usually have a great deal in common, which provides the potential to keep a relationship passionate and strong. Cancer and Scorpio like a comfortable home and will enjoy buying things together to create that space. Scorpio strives for power while Cancer likes security. Since they are both focused on their family and their home, they complement each other well.

Leo: Aries, Gemini, Libra and Sagittarius

Aries: Both are Fire Signs, that are competitive, so they both want to be in charge. This may either create a lot of passion or a lot of conflict. Both can be proud, impatient and dominant. Since Leo is a flirt and needs to be adored, Aries may get annoyed or bored with this.

Gemini: This union will be playful, hopeful, and high-spirited. Since Leo is dramatic and creative, Gemini will be satisfied with the mental stimulation from the pair. But, even though Leo is also a flirt, they may not like Gemini's desire to also do so. And if Gemini believes that Leo is trying to exhibit too much control over the relationship, conflict may erupt. Their differences in approaching a problem – intellectual versus instinctual – may cause some arguments as well.

Libra: An agreeable love match. Since they are two signs apart, they will have a deep understanding. Libra's harmony will counterbalance Leo's energy. Libra's charm and tact can also help to temper Leo's more direct and acerbic personality.

Sagittarius: Dynamic and full of life, this couple is fun to be around. Each encourages the other to reach for the stars. Both extremely social, they will want to be the leaders in their group of friends.

Virgo: Capricorn and Taurus

Capricorn: Virgo will love Capricorn's intensity while Capricorn will adore Virgo's attention to detail and intuition. A smart and very rational pairing. Their foundation will lay both of their realistic approach and a need for material security. Neither will let their emotions get the better of them and will exhibit admirable dedication to achieving goals.

Taurus: Practical is the key word here. Since Virgo is cautious by nature, any relationship between the two may take some time to develop. Both enjoy the finer things in life, but will work hard to earn them. Virgo's quick mind will complement Taurus' strength and dedication.
But Virgo's thoughts may lead to criticism and this may weigh too heavily on Taurus. And Taurus' stubborn nature may be a stumbling block for Virgo. Each must learn to not be quite so serious.

Libra: Leo and Sagittarius

Leo: Two signs apart in the Zodiac makes them a delightful pair. Libra's harmony will balance Leo's energy. Each will appreciate the contrasting aspects of the other and benefit from them. For example, Leo's more caustic and direct personality will be smoothed by Libra's good manners and charm. Leo will help Libra make decisions while Libra will help more whims.

Sagittarius: With signs that are two signs apart in the Zodiac, this is a harmonious romance. Libra appreciates art and beauty; Sagittarius is always searching for more experiences and knowledge. Exploring an art museum in a new town is a terrific first date. The relationship will stay in its romantic stage longer as this pair will keep things fresh and exciting. Libra may get their feelings hurt occasionally when Sagittarius speaks without thinking. And Sagittarius may feel a little boxed in emotionally. But Libra's diplomacy will smooth things over quickly.

Scorpio: Pisces and Scorpio

Pisces: Both water elements, they have a lot of respect for each other. Pisces is gentle and kind which Scorpio will greatly admire. Idealistic, Pisces can sometimes withdraw into their own selves, a trait which Scorpio will understand. Scorpio may help Pisces to turn some of their dreams into reality. Minor conflict may occur if Scorpio gets too dedicated to material possessions and doesn't give Pisces the freedom to devote to charity. Long-term ambitions are almost completely dissimilar, but knowing this, they can work together to form a plan for the both of them.

Scorpio: A perfect passionate storm. May become obsessed with one another and the relationship will advance quickly. It will be an all-or-nothing proposition – the best relationship ever, or the most destructive. The intensity of the love match makes their shared power unconquerable as long as their combined energy and passion aren't self-destructing.

Sagittarius: Aquarius, Aries, Leo and Libra

Aquarius: This will be a unique and creative union. A close friendship will exist underneath their good love pairing, even if their spirit of competition will need close monitoring. With the signs two signs apart on the Zodiac, there is excellent rapport. These two will enjoy good times together since they are both idealistic and excited about life. With both signs valuing their independence, they will work together to ensure they are a team. Communication would be a key to happiness.

Aries: These two have a lot in common and are very compatible. Always ready for a new adventure, they desire lots of life experiences. But, since they rush into things and overlook details, they may suffer some accidents. Their biggest challenge may be making the relationship into a long-term arrangement. Both will forgive and forget quickly, so they won't hold long-term grudges.

<u>Leo</u>: Sagittarius and Leo are very dynamic and live life to the fullest. Each one will encourage their partner to soar. People will enjoy being with this couple, as they are both charming and charismatic. Leo will want to be in control while Sagittarius will want to examine the nuances and plan an approach.

<u>Libra</u>: Two signs apart on the Zodiac, this pair exists in agreement. Sagittarius is always in search of learning and Libra has an appreciation for pretty things. Since Sagittarius likes to travel and explore, Libra will be a good companion for new sights. Their relationship will remain in the romance stage longer as they are both optimistic and will work to keep things exciting. Libra is a diplomat and will work to resolve any conflict and both are rather quick to forgive any slight rather quickly.

Capricorn: Pisces, Scorpio, Taurus, and Virgo

Pisces: This may seem to be a case of "opposites attract," and this relationship may develop slowly and will get stronger over time. They are very honest with each other and devoted to the relationship. Capricorn will appreciate Pisces' sweet nature; and Pisces will be attracted to Capricorn's wittiness and stubbornness. Difficulties may occur if Capricorn dominates Pisces's sensitive side, but Pisces should understand that this is just Capricorn's style, and not a personal attack. The best part is their unique blend of temperaments.

Scorpio: As neither sign is quick to open their hearts, this relationship may take awhile to get off the ground. But, once they are comfortable with each other and trust they will have an intense connection of loyalty and friendship. Capricorn, capable and stable, will help to calm Scorpio's hot-headed temperament. They must not be too stable or placid as Scorpio enjoys intense emotional connection. And those emotions may teach Capricorn to look below the surface of life. As goal-oriented signs, if they make their relationship a goal, there will be a success.

Taurus: Realistic, dependable and conservative, these two signs seem to be two peas in a pod. However, at their core, they can seem quite different. Capricorn can see Taurus as too lazy since they are not as focused on career and success. Taurus can find Capricorn a little too restrained and traditional. But, if they can meet in the middle and each learn a little something from the other, the relationship will benefit. Their similar values may be enough to bridge any gap.

Virgo: A strong foundation of a union of brains. These signs are smart, realistic, and rational. They expect a lot of themselves and out of others. Capricorn will respect Virgo's intuition while Virgo will appreciate Capricorn's intensity. Both enjoy material security and won't let their emotions get the better of them. Dedicated to each other with similar goals, their mutual interests can make this a relationship with a future.

Aquarius: Gemini and Libra

Gemini: Seems like a perfect match: Geminis love ideas and Aquarius is usually full of wonderfully visionary ideas. Both with a strong need for independence and lots of energy, they will recognize and respect that quality in their partner. Conflict may arise if Gemini seems too flighty for fast-moving Aquarius; or if Aquarius seems too stubborn for Gemini. They are great at working together and will be a veritable think-tank for great ideas.

Libra: These two signs seem to connect on a higher mental plane, sharing a love of culture, people, art and beauty. With a similar level of commitment to a relationship, they will not be unbalanced by one partner being more needy than the other. Energetic and enthusiastic, they will enjoy being together and experiencing new things, especially if that activity can bring a positive change to the world. Aquarius, the most progressive mind of the Zodiac, when combined with diplomatic Libra, can be a great addition to any worthy cause.

Pisces: Cancer and Scorpio

Cancer: A balance of the practical and the spiritual. Cancer can help dreamy Pisces bring their dreams to life; Pisces can offset Cancer's practicality with a little daydreaming.

Conflict may occur if Cancer, who loves material possessions, doesn't understand or respect the Spartan lifestyle that their Pisces partner prefers. Their shared emotional connection may overcome any differences in goals and lifestyles. They will rotate on the role of teacher or student as both have a great capacity for compassion. Their emotions will teach their partners and the world.

<u>Scorpio</u>: Two water elements, these signs are intuitive and in touch with human nature. This partnership will be a blending of mind and heart. Scorpio's tendency to be secretive may be a good sign to pair with Pisces, as they will understand having their own need to withdraw into their own minds occasionally. Scorpio may help Pisces to turn dreams into reality and provide the foundation for the relationship to be built on. Pisces are more in tune with emotions and spirituality making them be able to show Scorpio a world of sympathy and kindness. If they can overcome what may seem like different long-term plans, this can be a very rewarding romance with a profound connection and commitment.

Chapter 3: Finding Yourself through Your Zodiac and Growing on a Spiritual Level

Astrology is considered by most people to be a superstitious guide to everyday life. But, in reality, it can be a very deep subject. If used only for guidance in mundane matters, you will not be utilizing astrology for all of its teachings. Philosophically and mathematically speaking, astrology is a vast network of information that can provide profound understanding. Historically, astrology was used primarily as a guide to spiritual development and was considered a divine science. Although a science, once an astrologer begins to make predictions and classifications of human behavior, it crosses into a psychological or metaphysical field. If those predictions are reliable and unchanging, then this further emphasizes the metaphysical aspects of the practice. Scientifically, there is not proven, causal relationship between any one given planet and the way someone falls in love. However, it can be a technique for interpreting a situation in relation to the universe as a whole. Astrology can provide the clues to discovering the meaning of any situation and the way the factors of any situation operate. This can be the reason that people who struggle with traditional spiritual rules can turn to astrology. Everyone is seeking answers to "why" and "how," and the signs may provide guidance without restriction.

According to a New York Post article, more than half of the millennial generation believes in astrology as a science. This is compared to only eight percent of the Chinese public. This can include other metaphysical services such as tarot card, aura reading, astrology, mediums, and palmistry. One theory is that the lack of structure in the field of astrology may be exactly what is desirable about it for them.

However, with astrology, humankind can study the influence of the planets and further investigate the link between all aspects of creation. Astrology is meant to assist with everyone's inner journey, allowing people to become more aware of how the universe can impact all aspects of existence. The relation of the planets and stars to the human existence, mind, and body is very subtle.

A person is born on a specific time and day and is established into an astrological sign, house, cusp or other designation. To fully reflect on the traits and predilections of those under that category, you can investigate and strive to completely understand your relationship with the universe. This can be especially useful by raising your awareness of the past and the potential of the future, finessing your inner attunement with God. However, approaching astrology as a superstition can limit the use of this information and change this resource to a passive dependence on fate while you wait for the planets or stars to shift positions. Some people believe that religion and astrology cannot exist together as God is the only one who can have power or influence over your lifestyle, personality, and future. Under this argument, if you are spiritual and can actually commune with God to receive answers on how you should behave and what your path is in life, there is no need for anything like astrology to guide you. Others believe that astrology can simply give you more information about your journey in this world and also with God, giving you further understanding and knowledge of yourself and those you interact with every day. Or it may separate from spirituality completely and use astrology as a way to dissect and study the universe as it exists only through a cycle of cosmic principles and energy. Any one of these approaches is a personal interpretation that everyone must make on their own.

It can be argued that the use of astrology as a superstition can make someone into an automaton who is slavishly dependent on readings of the stars and positions of the planets. Those that argue this position indicate that allegiance to the Creator of the universe is the one true way and should be lead by the spirit and not by the material world. By delving deeply into your own divine nature, you may uncover deeper levels within yourself that will enable you to rise above all karmic realities.

Those in support of using astrology believe that the zodiac signs were developed by God to reveal information and teach us. Since God created the stars and planets and the zodiac signs are based on those, there is a synergy that exists. Awareness and correction of our weaknesses and strength can give us a greater sense of our behavior and tune us into improving.

Taoism of Chinese culture is very closely associated with the zodiac. This religion believes that things in space can change a person's destiny and constellations and space can be used to show that future. The sun was an integral part of the calculations of the zodiac as well. Many signs are discussed as being a "yin" or "yang" sign, and this originates with Taoism. This represents any two opposing principles of the universe and is the basis for how everything works. When combined, the yin-yang can change the characteristics of the twelve zodiac animals.

Another example of a religion that ties to the zodiac is Buddhism. Legend tells how Buddha chose all of the animals for the zodiac. This religion is popular in Chinese culture and has had a big effect on how the zodiac was structured and the role it now plays in modern-day religion. But there are some historical and astrological evidence that the religions of Christianity, Judaism, Paganism, Hinduism, Taoism, Zoroastrianism, Jainism, Islam, and Buddhism all share some similarities with each other and astrological science.

- Christianity: The central belief of Christianity is that Jesus Christ is the Son of God and the Savior (Messiah). Christians have faith that Jesus was anointed as the savior of humanity by God and believe that Jesus' life and crucifixion were the fulfillment of prophecies contained in the Old Testament.

- Judaism: This is characterized by the belief of one transcendent God who revealed himself to Moses, Abraham, and the Hebrew prophets and by a religious life in accordance with rabbinic traditions and scripture.

- Paganism: This is a polytheistic religion that focuses on sensual pleasures and material goods. This is a movement to revive nature-worshiping, pre-Christian religion and other nature-based spiritual paths. This definition may be a larger umbrella term for similar groups such as Wicca and Neo-Druidism.

- Hinduism: The major beliefs and principles of Hinduism include the four aims of human life (Purusartha) specifically: Artha (work, prosperity, and wealth), Dharma (duties/ethics), Kama (passions/desires), and Moksha (freedom and liberation) along with Karma, Samsara, and Yogas.

- Taoism: A Chinese philosophy denoting the fundamental or true nature of the world with a selflessness and simplicity in conformity with the Tao. A life expressing the essence of spontaneity and leading a life of non-purposive action. Taoism arose around the same time as Confucianism.

- Zoroastrianism: Zoroaster taught the existence of demons, angels, and saviors, similar ideas which can also be found in Judaism, Christianity, and Islam. The Avesta is their sacred text and contains rituals, hymns, and spells against demons.

- Jainism: This is a non-theistic religion founded in the 6th century BC in India as a reaction against the orthodox teachings of Brahmanism, and still practiced there. The Jain religion teaches reincarnation and salvation by perfection through those successive lives, and doing no harm to living creatures, and is noted for its ascetics.

- Islam: Someone who follows or practices Islam is called a Muslim which is a monotheistic, Abrahamic religion. Muslims read the Quran as their holy book and consider it to be the verbatim word of Allah as revealed to the Islamic messenger and prophet, Muhammad.
-
- Buddhism: This is a religion where truth is paramount. A practitioner is always striving to achieve the state of truth and is aware of the suffering of this world. People who worship Buddhism don't believe that their actual god is Buddha. To them, Buddha is a representation as a human who achieves the enlightenment phase and sees how the mind truly works. They believe that a person changers when they have this knowledge. Achieving total enlightenment is called "nirvana."

Under the teachings of astrology, each of the signs have a way that they prefer living their lives and a type of belief system that speaks to them. In general, Air and Water signs are more spiritual, and Fire and Earth signs are more committed to a structured or specific religion. Each sign has different needs and abilities and may be more inclined to follow a spiritual belief system that connects to their basic outlook.

Aries: A Fire Sign ruled by the planet Mars may need a physical spiritual practice, but with control. Yoga may be suited to this temperament, especially those types that are more energetic or vigorous in practice.

Taurus: An Earth Sign ruled by artistic Venus that brings out a gentle and creative approach to life. Most Taurus enjoy being in nature. This may lead them to feel a close connection to the Pagan religion. The celebrations throughout the year combining the spiritual with feasts and celebrations will speak directly to the heart of a Taurus. Having a close connection to the planet makes anyone under this Earth sign more enthusiastic.

Gemini: The planet Mercury rules this Air Sign. Gemini needs to be constantly busy mentally. This allows them to be more open to alternative approaches and spiritual discipline. The practice of mindful meditation, a Buddhist tradition, may help to quiet the mind and bring peace. With too much taxing the mind, the body can suffer as the nervous system can be pushed into insomnia and anxiety. The practice of turning off the brain and focusing on deeper connections is a great way to deal with stress.

Cancer: A Water Sign influenced by the Moon, Cancer individuals can display a higher level of psychic awareness than other signs, especially if they have a history or family ancestors with similar abilities. Psychic pursuits, clairvoyance, aura readings, and other similar fields may tune into the abilities and penchant of Cancer.

Leo: A Fire Sign ruled by the Sun, Leos have a lot of energy and need to be active daily. A spiritual practice that may appeal to them and which suits their temperament would be Tai Chi. Tai Chi is strongly linked to the Chinese philosophy and martial arts. It adds strength to the posture, deepens the breathing, and has many health benefits. Leos will enjoy Tai Chi classes more over practicing alone as those will ad a social aspect to it as well.

Virgo: An Earth Sign ruled by Mercury, Virgos need to be careful to engage in regular exercise and follow a diet. As their nervous system is an area of concern, they will benefit from regular practice. Alternative sources such as spiritual healing, aura reading, or Reiki can be beneficial to this sign. Essentially, when participating in a spiritual activity, Virgos need activities that do not overly use their minds but can bring themselves out. It is assumed that among the twelve signs, Virgo is the natural healer. Virgo likes to give advice and service, so any spiritual or religious practice that includes doing good works would be close to their heart. However, any spiritual practice for a Virgo should allow them to recharge their mental batteries.

Libra: An Air Sign ruled by Venus, balance is their trademark. The study of auras might interest a Libra. Auras are the field that surrounds the physical body and are typically different colors which can display physical health, emotional well-being, and spirituality. The study and recognition of auras may allow a Libra to better understand the actions of others and teach them how to become more balanced when dealing with the other people in their lives. In turn, this may help them to build better relationships with people around them.

Scorpio: A Water Sign ruled by Pluto, a spiritual journey will come as second nature to a Scorpio. During their lifetime, they may investigate a number of religions until they identify closely with one. With a drive to understand their life path and human psychology, they may experiment divination practice with Tarot to address the choices people face every day and properly decide on options that will make them move forward. The mysterious nature of the Tarot may appeal to a Scorpio to delve into the hidden aspects of the universe and life and to further understand the reason of why people live and thrive on Earth.

Sagittarius: A Fire Sign ruled by Jupiter, this sign is known as the philosopher of the zodiac. They may be drawn to philosophy or a teaching role in whatever religion they choose. As they enjoy studying and exploring new ways of thinking and then sharing those words of wisdom, they may indeed venture into being a spiritual leader. Their journey into spirituality may involve Christianity, Hindu, Buddhism, or other alternative religion.

Capricorn: An Earth Sign ruled by Saturn, although a materialistic sign, Capricorn does have the spiritual virtues that are required for a spiritual journey. Individuals in this sign need a spirituality that is going to last, combining both the need for being alone and spiritual advancement. Although less widely known, one option may be Shamanism. A Shaman alters the state of consciousness to communicate with the power of animals and the spirit world. Shamanism originates in central and northern Asia. This ancient and powerful spiritual practice takes time to learn, which will ensure a connection with Capricorn.

Aquarius: An Air Sign ruled by Uranus, Aquarius is always looking up at the stars and to the future. Those under this sign may indeed be inclined to astrology. For those under this sign, astrology may be the key to self-understanding. Following astrology and finding the pattern through the planets and constellations may be a source of guidance to an Aquarius. Once this pattern is revealed, an Aquarian delves into a journey of joy and fulfillment and can take that lost knowledge to others.

Pisces: A Water Sign ruled by Neptune, a Pisces personality constitutes their journey through their life and their spirituality. As the last sign of the zodiac, the Pisces understands it is only a small distance away to the next world. Pisces can contact the dead and possesses incredible physic awareness. The Pisces need to learn self discipline by energy cleaning and meditation. They are very sensitive with the surroundings and those that they come in with. To help steady their energy, it is best to give them some time to recuperate and be creative. This can lead them to a number of spiritual pursuits that connect them to that awareness such as reiki healing, aura cleansing, meditation, and more.

Chapter 4: How You Can Strengthen Your Relationships and Friendships by Reading the Zodiac Signs

When you explore astrology and see what traits and tendencies are common to each of the zodiac signs. You can then be prepared when dealing with friends, coworkers, managers, lovers and potential mates. Knowing the traits of others can help us to be better prepared to accept the flaws and all. And that's really what most people would like to experience – being accepted. As such, we can use the following information to prepare for interactions with a certain zodiac sign in our lives.

An ARIES BOSS: They are born leaders, but can be demanding. They provide clear instructions that are explicit. Aries can enjoy making decisions and seeing their plans implemented. They like individuality for themselves and others.

An ARIES EMPLOYEE: They are good at following rules and taking direction from supervisors. But they will quickly recognize any shortcomings of their supervisors. They will be quiet and hard-working until some small item sets them off. Aries employees will be full of suggestions to improve how things are done.

An ARIES ROMANCE: Noted for their honesty. They love close involvement with their romantic partner. But they also need a partner with lots of energy to keep up with them. Aries partners can be independent but will want daily contact. Make sure to never call them needy, but they feel the need to be very connected to their partners. Make sure to listen to their needs, feelings, and advice.

An ARIES SPOUSE: Honesty is prized; an Aries will expect to be forgiven if they stray. Since they are career-oriented, they may lean more towards their career than family. A spouse will need to ensure things run smoothly at home. However, they are not exceptional housekeepers/cleaners.

An ARIES FRIEND: Friends are faithful but may only contact their friends as frequently as every few months. Your Aries friend will be busy and may not have a lot of time to interact. If you are an Aries' oldest friend, you may even get included in family celebrations making you that important.

An ARIES PARENT: Sometimes too involved in their children's lives, Aries parents have strong ethical beliefs and will not be very tolerant of breaking rules. They must remember to allow their kids to try, fail and learn.

An ARIES CHILD: Childhood is a very big part to Aries, as long as the parents don't over-burden their children with adult responsibilities. An Aries child is best left alone with the security to express themselves without being condemned.

A TAURUS BOSS: The Taurus boss can be bossy, but will stay behind the scenes as long as their employees are well trained. They will take the time to explain their expectations. All rules will be minimal, but the rules are also considered to be concrete.

A TAURUS EMPLOYEE: Very work-oriented, but sometimes more oriented on personal comfort, making their progress on a task is slower. They are good at procrastination and will respond better to a gentle reminder than sharp orders.

A TAURUS ROMANCE: A Taurus tends to be possessive and may treat a partner as something that belongs to them. However, they will see this as a positive reflection of how much they love you. Conflict may arise if you try to be independent and not agree with everything your Taurus asks.

A TAURUS SPOUSE: Taurus spouse is caring, devoted, dependable, stable, and usually the dominant partner. They enjoy being the head of the household. They like to make most of the big decisions. Taurus spouses can procrastinate but once they decide, there is not stopping them. They love pleasure: food, sex, and other sensual pleasures.

A TAURUS FRIEND: They are always faithful and will help as much as possible. But they may not be the best source of useful advice. They see things in black and white, so their vision may not be skewed. Fun to be with, Taurus friends enjoy entertainment. But you must be careful not to take advantage of their generous nature.

A TAURUS PARENT: They love being parents as they are nurturers. Taurus parents enjoy large families. They struggle to love unconditionally, so they may not be able to support their children unless certain conditions are met. Consequently, their children may not trust promises or generosity.

A TAURUS CHILD: A child of this Sign can be of a serious nature. Since they interpret things literally, they will expect parents and authority figures to keep their promises. They will be a complex combination of talking and silence; active and lazy; excited and aloof – which makes their moods hard to read moods. They will be unhappy if they do not have their own stuff. A Taurus child will share their toys, but only on their terms.

A GEMINI BOSS: A Gemini boss is comfortable with giving orders and coordinating. They like being part of a team as it allows them to share experiences. They are not born leaders, preferring to be a "hands off" leader. Gemini is very good at delegating but likes to have the final say.

A GEMINI EMPLOYEE: They love to be busy, and they are very good at multi-tasking. They love to think up new approaches to old projects. But Geminis get bored easily and may lack follow-through on long-term projects. They are usually particularly adroit manually.

A GEMINI ROMANCE: Will definitely add excitement to your life, but also some uncertainty. It may be difficult to predict their moods. Gemini may sometimes flake on appointments. They will be fascinating but may also be aggravating.

A GEMINI SPOUSE: They will need individuality and freedom. They may create problems with stability in the marriage. A Gemini spouse may get double standards in place when they feel they deserve more freedom than their spouses. Usually, don't think what they are doing is ever wrong morally. Must have a strong spouse that stands up to them.

A GEMINI FRIEND: They are more fun to be around when things are going well. They are susceptible to stress out when it comes to emergencies. If you want to have a good time, invite along a Gemini. They will provide lots of chatter, so be prepared to listen.

A GEMINI PARENT: They will offer their children a wide variety of interests and stimulation. They are good parents when they are interested and engaged. They enjoy their role as the family leader. But they may be too preoccupied with the stuff in their own minds to be a caretaker whole-heartedly all the time, so kids must be prepared to take care of themselves. Geminis are susceptible to worry and stress.

A GEMINI CHILD: Needs lots of parental input. They will display a lot of interest over a lot of different subjects. They should have a great deal of stimulation to keep them engaged. They will range from an easy child to a very challenging one based on possible stimulation and moods.

A CANCER BOSS: They are very particular about how things get done. They can be demanding. They want things to run smoothly and they like their dominance to be unquestioned. Rules are not as important as the team but do not underestimate the dominant qualities of a Cancer boss.

A CANCER EMPLOYEE: They are best at a desk job if they are not interrupted, they can produce a lot of paperwork. A Cancer employee possesses a good loyalty to the company they work for. They will play things close to the vest, watching, listening, and learning. Thus, their opinions are worth listening to.

A CANCER ROMANCE: They like steady, reliable relationship. Since they like habits, they like their partners to be available to them on a regular basis. They will count on them for everything. A Cancer partner can be cuddly as long as they are getting their way. If not, they may come across as crabby or withdrawn. They are very self-protective.

A CANCER SPOUSE: They like to have security at home. Since a Cancer spouse will spend a lot of time at home, they like their house "just so." They may spend too much money on home furnishings or improvements.

A CANCER FRIEND: They will work to keep their friends to themselves and not share. They want to know you are their best friend. They are good listeners, but will probably not share a lot of their own personal information.

A CANCER PARENT: Loving and caring parents that are both affectionate and protective. But, a Cancer parent can sometimes become over-protective, it can be a hard lesson for them to learn on how to let go a little.

A CANCER CHILD: Can become overly dependent on their parents. They need security and a great deal of support and guidance from their parents. Developing their own independence is a Cancer child's challenge.

A LEO BOSS: Is a born leader. The Leo enjoys being the head of the company. Leo bosses are fair as long as their authority is not being challenged. They believe they are simply trying to stand up for the working conditions of their employees. They take great pride in their work.

A LEO EMPLOYEE: Will be faithful to the company to the point of becoming a workaholic. They will stick faithfully to a job or a task. However, they will be resistant to change. Ambition will often push a Leo up the corporate ladder.

A LEO ROMANCE: Your girlfriend/boyfriend will be committed, supportive, and enthusiastic. But try not to impinge on their ambitious career plans; never make them choose between their relationship and career path. Although they hate to see a relationship end, they will have the confidence to move on with someone new.

A LEO SPOUSE: They are loyal, but may not remain faithful if their spouse seems distant. In order to be happy in marriage, Leo needs to be treated like royalty and put up on a pedestal. Since Leos are good at acting, they can pretend to be happily married for years just for the sake of the children involved, family or status.

A LEO FRIEND: They are excellent at making friends. Their loyalty and devotion are marks of their good friendship. They are not overly needy, so they can do without contact on a regular basis. However, when contacted, they prefer an in-person, close-up check-in rather than a phone call or text.

A LEO PARENT: Fiercely protective of their children, but they may go overboard as they think they always know better. Since their careers are important, they may not always be present as a parent. Leo parents may lean heavily on daycare, preschools, grandparents, and other assistants in child care.

A LEO CHILD: Will feel that caregivers are lucky to have them in their lives. They are confident and strong and self-assured. They will be accomplished in what activities they participate in. May not be inclined to academia, but will contribute to politics, activities, and sports.

A VIRGO BOSS: Realistic and practical, so results will be important to this boss. Data supporting any position or argument will greatly improve your chances of convincing them in an argument. Emotions do not play well, so stick with logic. A Virgo boss will not appreciate wasting time.

A VIRGO EMPLOYEE: They will take their work seriously. Dependable and trustworthy, they can sometimes be a little dull. Since they are private people, work can be a good social outlet, so much so that they frequently find that a co-worker ends up being their best friend.

A VIRGO ROMANCE: They are very good at planning. Their talents are best utilized by putting them in charge of setting up the yearly vacation or complicated outings. But, they may put more focus into the relationship rather than the person they are actually with.

A VIRGO SPOUSE: Good at marriage and homemaking but can get too insistent on order. This may drive their spouse crazy. In contrast to their need for order, their personal space may be rather sloppy (to you, but there is an order in the mess for them). They shine when it comes to emergency situations.

A VIRGO FRIEND: Supportive and helpful, they seem to intuitively know when you need them. They may seem needy, but they have trouble asking for help. Constant contact is not necessary, but make sure you check in periodically.

A VIRGO PARENT: They like making rules and are big on structure. This may create conflict as the child seeks independence, especially during the power struggle of adolescence.

A VIRGO CHILD: They are dutiful but resentful and may grow out of control if they feel unappreciated. The reward for helpfulness should be considered as they respond to this. They have highly judgmental and critical side. There will be long-term issues if the parent doesn't keep promises made to the Virgo child.

A LIBRA BOSS: They need to believe they are well-liked by their employees. Sometimes, they make them focus more on popularity than performance. Those who know that may manipulate that weakness.

A LIBRA EMPLOYEE: They prefer to work alone since they may have problems concentrating when surrounded by distractions. They can be perfectionists. Colleagues may value them for their understanding nature.

A LIBRA ROMANCE: They are choosy about who is on their arm: what they look like, sound like, and behave like. They expect to be treated well, but may not consider reciprocating. Problems arise when Libras are unhappy, so issues should be addressed immediately.

A LIBRA SPOUSE: Good at arranging the social life, but more interested in their immediate family than any extended relatives. Usually, they tend to be the head of the family. Pleasing their spouses is very important. If their spouses don't seem happy, they may become depressed or frustrated.

A LIBRA FRIEND: Friendships are usually limited in length and can end quickly. Intense relationships but friends can feel dumped without reason.

A LIBRA PARENT: Sensitive about their social standing, they want their children to look good and be the "right" child. They may be involved in planning the right course for their children (classes, activities, friends, etc.). They will carefully monitor school activities and grades, even going so far as to take credit for their child's accomplishments.

A LIBRA CHILD: Obedient but demanding, and they want to be the center of attention. A Libra child will want to be rewarded, recognized, and appreciated with love and attention. As a performer, they are a constant source of entertainment. They have creative talents.

A SCORPIO BOSS: A powerful, dominant, serious, dedicated, hard-driving boss who sets high standards. They do not accept excuses and do not like their authority being questioned.

A SCORPIO EMPLOYEE: Will get the work done if they are let alone to do so. They have their own way of doing things. They are loyal to the company and will do their best for their duty. They can get aggressive when unfairly criticized.

A SCORPIO ROMANCE: Can be both possessive and jealous. They want 100% of your attention on them. If they feel this is waning, they can become withdrawn or depressed. They feel like they give a lot, so they deserve a lot and that their spouse should feel lucky to have them. Territorial and protective, they can display concern for their loved ones.

A SCORPIO SPOUSE: Loyal, but not always faithful. They can be secretive, so typically does not share information with friends and family. They love the home and spend a lot of time there.

A SCORPIO FRIEND: Very selective about who their friends are. So if you are the friend of a Scorpio, then feel like you have been honored with being chosen. They are not very needy, so will not need constant contact, but will contact you when they want to go out for some fun. However, the friendship may be structured on their terms. A mutable sign may get along with them easier as they can "go with the flow" or changes in the mood and emotions.

A SCORPIO PARENT: Usually set up their household with very strict rules. They will be direct with their children but will have a set of chores and responsibilities the child must follow regularly. They are very proud of their children. They want them to look their best for family events, social obligations, and school. They will see their child's appearance and behavior as a reflection of their parenting skills. Since they can be a little uncompromising, it is better that only one parent in the family is a Scorpio.

A SAGITTARIUS BOSS: Big on independence, they are not always suited to being a boss. Employees may have a hard time keeping up, as the Sagittarius boss can go off in their own direction. They may not communicate clearly to their team as they are not very good at being team players.

A SAGITTARIUS EMPLOYEE: Can be dedicated and hard working, but need to be monitored closely to ensure they are staying on track.

A SAGITTARIUS ROMANCE: This relationship will be intense and passionate. They will bring out the best in their partners. As they are not good with dealing with disappointment, they may fall into depression if things aren't going well. Relaxed with a good humor, they enjoy the pleasures of life.

A SAGITTARIUS SPOUSE: Capable of struggle to balance home and career since they want to make their mark on the world. They may count on their spouses to take over a lot of the responsibilities around the home. When married to another power sign, they may benefit from having a housekeeper or help around the house.

A SAGITTARIUS FRIEND: Fun to be with, they are usually upbeat and keep their own troubles to themselves. To promote intimacy, you will have to push to discuss their feelings and situation. Since they tend to be overly optimistic, a true friend may have to talk some truth to them.

A SAGITTARIUS PARENT: Very giving and want to improve their household with beauty and devotion. So, they may be more inclined to indulge kids with pets. They enjoy parenting because of love, not because of some sense of duty or responsibility.

A SAGITTARIUS CHILD: Difficult, almost impossible to control. They love freedom and will break the rules. If they have a big personality parent, then big show-downs will happen. They thrive on challenges and love being the underdog who wins.

A CAPRICORN BOSS: As they are dominant, they want to be followed and obeyed without question. They would not like being out performed or overshadowed by an employee. They may not want to advance any further in the company, but will want to hang on to their boss status as long as possible.

A CAPRICORN EMPLOYEE: Hard working and dedicated, they are also ambitious. They will be loyal to a company only when the company's interest does not conflict with their own. The quality of their work will be very high.

A CAPRICORN ROMANCE: Typically faster at jumping into the physical side of a relationship and then focusing on getting to know the other person on a deeper level. They prefer to develop deeper relationships and will not waste time or energy on people without a future.

A CAPRICORN SPOUSE: Need to be the dominant head of the family. They must be in control of everyone around them. They may impose unrealistic expectations on their spouse. But, for the sake of harmony, they should learn to back off occasionally.

A CAPRICORN FRIEND: Will be there for their friends during times of difficulties. Being the best friend of a Capricorn can be challenging. They will only let a few people in their lives into their emotional inner circle: spouse, best friend, and maybe a few family members.

A CAPRICORN PARENT: Big on authority and control, a Capricorn parent is protective. They take their rules very seriously. In order to maintain control over their children, they may withhold demonstrations of love.

A CAPRICORN CHILD: Act like miniature adults in their childhood, with a serious demeanor. They need to be respected or they will act out. With self-assurance, they know how to get what they want and may use emotional blackmail, guilt or manipulation to get it.

An AQUARIUS BOSS: Not suited to be a boss as they are impulsive and generally disinterested in power. But, can be fun to work with as they are of a generous nature. At times, they can be impatient with a quick temper.

An AQUARIUS EMPLOYEE: Will have their own unique way of completing a task but may get stuck in a rut on how they do things. They can be rebellious so they may not take orders well. But will bring levity to a group of co-workers.

An AQUARIUS ROMANCE: Will be faithful, but that may be in jeopardy if someone more interesting comes along. If you can stimulate them and satisfy their appetites, the relationship may last long term. The boyfriend/girlfriend of an Aquarius needs to be forgiving and self-assured.

An AQUARIUS SPOUSE: Devoted to the family. Once marriage is decided on, they will commit completely. It is very important to them to feel they are needed by their spouse and family. Although they will be away from home a lot because of work, they enjoy domestic bliss. Their good moods help to enhance interactions when they are home.

An AQUARIUS FRIEND: Friendship is very important to them, but will not be a stable friendship. Contact will be sporadic and conversation will focus more on the abstract, big picture items than on exchanging feelings or sharing.

An AQUARIUS PARENT: Frequently, an Aquarius will choose not to marry or have children. If they do go the family route, they will encourage their children to grow and explore. They are not possessive or over-protective and will push their children out of the next as early as possible. Freedom is vital to them until they feel their child is in danger.

An AQUARIUS CHILD: Insistent on doing their own way and may get difficult if forced to waver from that. They have a joyful nature and they will respond well to attention and understanding from their parent.

A PISCES BOSS: Excellent at being the boss. Money-making comes easy to them and they are equally good at protecting the money-making interests and abilities of their business.

A PISCES EMPLOYEE: Adaptable and can walk into almost any position and help out. Selfless, they will sacrifice their own needs for the good of the company. However, this may lead to some long term resentment. Best working conditions are the financial reward for a good performance.

A PISCES ROMANCE: Give their all into a relationship. As a girlfriend or boyfriend, they can be demanding, seductive, possessive, and passionate.

A PISCES SPOUSE: Family oriented, they enjoy spending lots of time at home. They are dedicated to raising a family even if that means transferring that parental impulse to a step-child, adopted child, niece/nephew, or other close family members. Pets can even become like children to them. They may become overprotective.

A PISCES FRIEND: They are tuned into their friends' feelings and needs. They are sensitive and respectful of feelings. They are good in times of need. Usually, they have a close circle of friends: quality over quantity. Their door is always open to their friends in need.

A PISCES PARENT: Dedicated to the personal growth and the welfare of their children. A Pisces parent will devote most of their energy into raising their kids when their kids are at home with them. They are both proud of their children and anxious about their well being. They may be fearful at times and need to encourage their child to be independent.

A PISCES CHILD: Soft and sweet or difficult – no middle ground. Their moods may be out of sync with their feelings and the feelings of those around them. They may have a melt-down if they feel misunderstood. They are fragile and sensitive and soft and sweet (when they feel happy, accepted and loved).

Chapter 5: Birthday Charts

A birth chart, also known as an astrology or natal chart, is a map of the planet's location in the exact moment of your birth. It can reveal the secrets of your unique personality and your path through life. The placement of the planets will show you the universal energy in place at the moment you were born on the planet and can provide a roadmap to better understanding your quirks, motives, interests, and journey.

A step beyond simply reading your daily horoscope, a birth chart will reveal hidden parts of yourself. This chart will show the connections between your personality and the placement of planets as each planet has a specific energy that will govern a portion of your life. Most horoscopes are based on your sun sign, but a birth chart will add in information about the placement of the moon, your rising sign, and more. This may show that you are a cusp sign, which means you may be suspended between the traits of two Signs.

To create an accurate birth chart, the exact date and time (down to the minute) of your birth will be necessary, and, if possible, the location as well. The location is important to determine what constellations and planets were visible in the sky at the time of birth. Two people born at the exact same time on January 30, 2017, one located in London and one in New York would have completely different birth charts.

The inner planets, sun, moon, Mercury, Venus, and Mars, directly impact our unique personalities and are specific to an individual's date and time of birth. The outer planets, Pluto, Neptune, Uranus, Saturn, and Jupiter, define your larger life themes and experiences that can be shared across generations. The outer planet significance is decided by the house they are in at the time of your birth. Houses one through six, deal with routine activities; houses seven through to 12 deal with matters more philosophical. Where the planet is in the house shows where we keep our energy and where our weaknesses and strengths lie.

The unique location of the planet in the house shows your Rising Sign (or ascendant). Your Rising Sign is the zodiac sign that was on the Eastern horizon when you were born. The Rising Sign makes the structure of your birth chart, showing your planetary chart ruler, the planet associated with your birth chart. Your Rising Sign also shows your external experiences, meaning how you are perceived by others and interact with the world.

The birth chart can show your celestial name, which is your cosmic name, connecting you to the language of the universe. Your "mandala" is your own personal celestial signature and can show you what your place is in the scheme of energy surrounding everyone.

There are a number of websites online that can provide you with a free birth chart, also check locally to see if a new age shop or other resources can provide a more complete horoscope and birth chart.

Chapter 6: Astrology and the 12 Cell Salts

Cell Salt remedies were founded in the late 1880s by Dr. Schuessler who analyzed the human cells' ash residue and discovered twelve inorganic mineral salts. He then hypothesized that these twelve elements are important in balancing cellular and leath activity. These cell salt remedies have been used around the world for over 120 years. The cell salts are used in building up an individual's constitutional health since cell salts can be useful in rebuilding the tissues and organs and balancing the excess and deficiencies. The cell salts stabilizes the remedy for homeopathy when it relapses. Cell Salts are taken generally four times a day but can be used more frequently, and for a long duration of time.

Cell Salts are divided into five (6) groups.

    1) Calcium group
    2) Sodium group
    3) Potassium group
    4) Magnesium group
    5) Iron group
    6) Silica

<u>How to Take the Cell Salts</u>

Again, Cell Salts are suggested to be taken three to four times per day or at least five times per week. They can be taken often as necessary in the case of acute conditions. They are taken typically by dissolving the tablets in the mouth or maintaining a liquid for 15 seconds in the mouth before swallowing the tablet to absorb it fully. Ten to fifteen minutes before and after taking the salts, eating and drinking should be avoided, except for water. There is no risk of overdosing like those off the regular mineral supplements because they are prepared homeopathically.

Cell Salts by Zodiac Sign

Firstly it is important to be aware that this is not 100% accurate and should be taken the same way you take your star sign: Positively and in your own special way that helps you grow as a person.

Capricorn — Calcium Phosphate

Capricorn rules part of the skeletal structure including bones, joints, knees, and teeth. Capricorns are susceptible to diseases around these areas. This can include osteoporosis, arthritis, tendonitis, knee problems and teeth problems.

Considered the nutritional Cell Salt, Calcium Phosphate, it is a major component of our bones. This is an important remedy for development and growth and an excellent Cell Salt to take with typical calcium supplement, as it will enhance the absorption of the supplement. Calcium Phosphate Cell Salts will help to remedy brittle bones and can help to accelerate healing if you have a broken bone. This Cell Salt can also be used to rub onto the gums during teething to alleviate pain or given during those painful growing spurts that children sometimes experience.

-
  Why you would need to take Calcium:
- Growth spurts, broken bones, osteoporosis, remineralization of teeth and teething in children.
- Sore throat.
- Feeling overwhelmed.

These salts are included in foods such as beetroots, avocados, buttermilk carrots, cheese, beans, parsley, linseed meal, milk, and peanuts.

Aquarius — Sodium Chloride

Aquarius is represented by a water-bearer and covers the lower legs, ankles, and the circulation system. Those under the Sign of Aquarius can be prone to problems with legs (torn ligaments, pulled muscles, cramps, and weak ankles), poor circulation, and high blood pressure.

Salt water's main ingredient is Sodium Chloride. Sodium and chloride ions are important in the extracellular fluid, as they help balance fluids moving in and out of cells. It is considered a major grief remedy on the emotional level. Physically, it helps to keep the correct balance of fluids in our bodies. People with a deficiency may crave salt or have an increased in thirst, their lips may crack, and may suffer from constipation. In contrast, those with an excess may have to take diuretics and have swelling in their hands and feet. This may help with instances of high blood pressure that is the result of the system being sensitive to salt levels.

Why you would need to take Sodium Chloride:

- Cold sores
- Balances fluids.
- Digestion problems with heartburn.
- Remedy for emotional grief, menopause or PMS symptoms.
- Hives.
- High blood pressure.

Foods containing this salt include: almonds, apples, celery, cheese (goat and Roquefort), egg yolks, goat cheese, lentils, onions, peaches, pecans, sauerkraut, spinach, Swiss chard, and tomatoes.

Pisces— Phosphate of Iron (Ferrous Phosphate)

Pisces rules the toes, feet, liver, general physique, and immune system. Pisces are susceptible to diseases like an impaired immune system, liver disorders, edema, gout, injuries to the toes and feet, and possibly addictions.

Iron Phosphate is useful in alleviating inflammation of all tissues of the body. It is the best treatment for inflammation out of the 12 Cell Salts, especially for people who are anemic. They are also the best homeopathic remedy for anemia. Iron is a very good treatment for a sore throat, low blood pressure, poor circulation, and will increase oxygenation in the blood.

Why you would need to take Iron:

- Inflammation anywhere in the body
- Fevers and a sore throat.
- Headache.
- Anemia.
- Increases circulation and blood oxygenation.

Foods containing this salt include beetroots, currants, dates, figs, grapes, lima beans, mushrooms, oranges, plums, prunes, raisins, spinach, and wheat bran.

Aries – Potassium Phosphate

As this is Zodiac's first sign, Aries oversees the head, brain, eyes, face, ears, nervous system, and the muscles. Aries is prone to migraines and other headaches, and brain disorders, this can include; mental illness, Parkinson's and Alzheimer's. Potassium Phosphate nurtures the brain and nerves. It is used to treat the side effects of emotional and physical stress, sleeplessness, headaches, exhaustion, poor memory, and irritability. This can work as nerve tonic and is great for students under stress from finals.

Why you would need to take Potassium Phosphate:

- Low energy levels
- Insomnia.
- Memory issues.
- Improve attention span and learning which is Great for students.
- Depression without an apparent cause.
- Calming anxiety and stress.

This salt is included in foods such as buttermilk, beans, beetroots, avocados, parsley, linseed meal, cheese, carrots, milk, and peanuts.

Taurus – Sodium Sulfate

As the second Sign of the zodiac, Taurus rules the throat and neck area including tonsils, vocal cords, and thyroid. Those under this Sign may suffer more from diseases like strep throat, tonsillitis, hyper and hypothyroidism, goiters, or neck injuries. Taurus also governs the liver and so liver disorders such as cirrhosis, hepatitis, or jaundice should be watched for closely.

Although this Cell Salt is to aid in treating the liver, it is not limited to just helping that organ. This Cell Salt can also alleviates irritability, depression, hepatitis, asthma, arthritis, photophobia, warts, and changes to the personality after a head injury. It is similar to arnica.

Why you would need to take Sodium Sulfate:

- Liver support.
- Asthma.
- Nausea.
- Support for depression, gloom and fear.

Foods containing this salt include: Brussel sprouts, cabbage, cauliflower, celery, egg yolks, kohlrabi, lettuce, milk, onions, radishes, and turnips.

Gemini — Potassium Chloride

Since Gemini is always on the move, they are more prone to worry and anxiety. They govern the shoulders, arms, hands, arms, ribs, lungs, nervous system, and blood. As such, Geminis are susceptible to nervous disorders, blood disorders, lung problems such as asthma, bronchitis, and also headaches.

They work with intercellular fluids, helping with sinusitis, ear infections and pain, swimmer's ear, vaginitis, and dandruff. They may help people who are traveling on a plane prevent sensitivity to pressure.

Why you would need to take Potassium Chloride
- Sinus infections.
- Sore throats.
- Mental issues: nervousness and anxiety.
- Ear pain, pressure or infections.
- Dandruff.

This salt is contained in foods such as cheese, egg yolks, lentils, radishes, spinach, sauerkraut, asparagus, carrots, and coconuts.

Cancer — Fluoride of Lime

Cancer governs the chest, digestive tract, womb, liver, and pancreas. Cancer is weak to digestive problems such as; ulcers, dyspepsia, and indigestion, breast problems, uterine disorders and liver maladies.

This salt is found in the elastic fibers of the skin, connective tissues, enamel of teeth, bones, and in the blood vessels. It is used to help alleviate varicose veins, cracks in the skin, sluggish circulation, loss of elasticity, loose/sensitive teeth, delayed dentition, the relaxation of tissues and blood vessels, varicose veins, hemorrhoids, bony tumors, and the displacements of organs.

Why you would need to take Fluoride of Lime:

- Loss of elasticity.
- Varicose veins.
- Hemorrhoids
- Slow circulation

This salt can be found in foods such as pineapple, kelp, goat cheese, garlic, beets, asparagus, and turnips.

Leo — Phosphate of Magnesia

Leos generally have good health, but concerns begin to arise when a Leo feels neglected. This Sign rules the upper back, blood, spleen, spine, and heart. Leos are susceptible to conditions like heart attacks, high blood pressure, arteriosclerosis, spinal cord injuries, eye disorders, blood diseases, and upper back problems.

Phosphate of Magnesium is very good for nerve pain. This Cell Salt can help with muscle cramps, back injuries, whiplash, neuralgia, sciatica, coughing, colic, toothaches, carpal tunnel syndrome, headaches, stomach cramps, Parkinson's, swimmer's ear, and more.

Why you would need to take Phosphate of Magnesium
- Coughing
- Nerve headaches.
- Carpal tunnel syndrome.
- Anti-spasmodic; cramps and whiplash.
- Will aid in magnesium absorption from supplements.

Foods containing this salt include almonds, asparagus, beechnuts, cabbage, cauliflower, cherries, figs, gooseberries, grapefruit, lemons, limes, oranges, peaches, and whole wheat.

Virgo — Potassium Sulfate

As Virgos may lean toward workaholic tendencies, they are prone to stress related illnesses. In addition, Virgo rules the lower digestive system such as the colon and small intestine, liver, and the sympathetic nervous system. Virgos are susceptible to digestive and intestinal problems that could involve ulcers, Crohn's, IBS, colitis, hemorrhoids, diverticulitis, and liver problems.

Potassium Sulfate is good for coughing, eczema, dandruff, ringworm, asthma, earaches, hot flashes, stiff joints, and tiredness.

Why you would need to take Potassium Sulfate:
- Hot flushes.
- Stiff joints.
- Stuffy nose, colds with yellow discharge.
- Detox support.
- Psoriasis, dry scalp, oily skin.
- Constipation.
- Fatigue.

This salt is included in foods such as onions, lettuce, Brussel sprouts, cabbage, celery, cucumbers, cauliflower, and tomatoes.

Libra – Sodium Phosphate

Libra rules the kidney, bladder, adrenals, and lower back. This Sign can be prone to diseases like kidney or bladder stones, incontinence, urinary tract infections, lumbago, lower backaches, and sprains.

Sodium Phosphate is found in intracellular fluid brain cells, nerves, and blood, muscles. This substance converts lactic acid into its byproducts. It can be used to help alleviate the symptoms of inflammatory rheumatism, headaches located on the top of the head, gout, pain over and inside the eyeballs, swollen joints, high sour breath, stiffness, cholesterol, lumbago, nausea, loss of appetite and habitual constipation.

Why you would need to take Sodium Phosphate:
- Gout
- Inflammation within the body.
- High cholesterol.
- Nausea and loss of appetite.
- Constipation.

Foods containing this salt include: asparagus, brown rice, buttermilk, citrus fruits juices, cottage cheese, eggs, lentils, parsley, tomato juice, vegetable greens, and whole wheat.

Scorpio — Sulfate of Lime

Scorpio governs the excretory organs, urinary, and reproductive. Scorpios are prone to diseases of the sexual system, reproductive and urinary tract infections.

Sulfate of lime occurs in nature as selenite or commercially known as "plaster of Paris,"alabaster, and gypsum. This substance is present in liver cells and connective
tissue.

Why you would need to take Sulfate of Lime

- Excessive sensitivity of nerves as well as cravings for fruit and acids
- Frontal headaches with nausea
- Pancreatic, liver and kidney disturbances
- Sore throats, colds
- Infection due to pus; pimples
- Cellular regeneration

Foods containing this salt include: Brussel sprouts, cabbage, cauliflower, celery, egg yolks, kohlrabi, lettuce, milk, onions, radishes, and turnips.

Sagittarius — Silica

Sagittarius governs the hips, liver, pelvis, and thighs, making them prone to hip problems, lumbago, and liver diseases.

Silica affects keratin and the fibrous tissues of the body and is important in getting the minerals in the body working correctly again. It can help to alleviate weakness and improve stamina. It can also help the body recover rapidly after surgery or illness, ease chronic ear infections in children and also act as a confidence booster.

Why you would need to take Silica:

- Scoliosis or weakness of the back.
- Improves hair, nails, skin, and connective tissue.
- Cleansing or eliminating waste.
- Lungs (asthma, shortness of breath, etc.)
- Alleviate weakness, improve stamina. Grogginess in the morning.
- Lack of self-confidence and courage.

This salt can be found in foods such as cucumber (with skins), raw cabbage, carrots, barley, endive, gooseberries, oats, peas, rye, spinach, strawberries, shredded wheat, and whole wheat.

Chapter 7: Extra Information

Other information that may be of use when researching your sign and the meaning of it all are the attributes and influences that may change the horoscope. There's are things such as the Quality of the signs, the Houses, Gemstones, Planets, Dates of the Cusps of the signs and the Greek and Roman Gods who represent the signs.

Quality of Signs:

Cardinal: This comes from the French for "hinge" (an item upon which something swings). Cardinal directions are North, South, East, and West. This also has to do with the changing seasons. Cardinal signs include: Aries, Cancer, Capricorn, and Libra. These are characterized by trailblazers, visionaries, enterprise, or starting things. Usually, you will find someone under a Cardinal Sign in the first place, although sometimes, quite by accident. They may take the long route around, but what they find along the trip will change things for the better. Once they have started something new, they may not have enough endurance to stick around long enough to see the project completed.

- Aries and Libra are equinox signs: This means that they balance the night and day. These Signs are both times of balance or of abrupt change.
- Cancer and Capricorn are solstice signs: The solstice is the times of the longest day and longest night, indicating that these are Signs representing times of extremes.

Cardinal Signs are associated with starting things, can be forceful and aggressive, and have the drive to accomplish new things.

- Aries will initiate change with urgency and high energy. They can't wait to do what their new project is.
- Cancer is emotionally assertive.
- Libra is balanced and will consider the viewpoints of others. They use communication to motivate others into action in order to make projects happen.

- Capricorn is practical and whatever action they take will be based on practical needs.

Fixed: These Signs are unchanging and securely placed. Fixed signs include: Aquarius, Leo, Scorpio, and Taurus. Characterized by dependability, stability, and firmness, they stick with how they know how to do tasks. Leadership is their specialty if they know what the rules are, but they can also take orders well and delegate responsibilities appropriately. At times, they may seem rigid. They are usually concerned with stabilizing an aspect of their lives or keeping things the same. Most change is aimed at keeping something the same, for example; clean house, healthy body and a steady job.

- Taurus does not like changes in the status of their wealth.
- Leo wants to appear impressive, keep personal power, and be creative.
- Scorpio wants to know what the emotions are of people around them and establish emotional stability.
- Aquarius seeks stability in their beliefs.

Mutable: These Signs are subject to change. Mutable signs include: Gemini, Pisces, Sagittarius, and Virgo. These signs are adaptable, always changing, experimental, but this may make them seem inconsistent. These Signs are very good at creativity.

- Geminis are focused on communication and the mind. They may allow any kind of change and adapt themselves to the environment around them.
- Virgo can be analytical and critical and may put an end to something that was thought to be true but was then revealed to be false.
- Sagittarius is a seeker of knowledge, bringing about a change from ignorance to knowledge.
- Pisces can change emotions into solidarity of all things.

Rising Signs: Rising Signs indicate the traits that you show when you are around people, in other words; the way you act. Your Sun sign reveals who you are at the core of your personality and your true character. Your Rising Sign is the sign that appear at the exact minute you were born over the eastern horizon. If you were born around sunrise, then your Rising sign is the same as your Sun sign. The Sun indicates what part of the zodiac the Sun was in.

The Astrological Houses

The horoscope was divided into twelve segments, the twelve houses, which represent the twelve sections of life:

- The First House: ascendant, representing the self, the people and their behavior, appearance, personality, ambitions, drive, energy, priorities, vitality, and deepest desires. This House is ruled by a lively, energetic, empire-building Mars and unique Aries.
- The Second House: all financial affairs, financial independence, earned income, the desire for stability, constructive talents, values, financial obligations, material possessions, a sense of security, and self-confidence. This House is ruled by the planet of love, Venus, and finances, and stable and practical Taurus.
- The Third House: travel, communication, the mind, intellectuals, trade, the media, writing, speech, education, ideas, relatives, and academic skills. This House is ruled by logical, talkative Mercury and adaptable Gemini.
- The Fourth House: the land, home, family, wealth, ethnic pride, personal and national soul. This House is ruled by both sentimental Cancer and the nurturing Moon.
- The Fifth House: creativity, self-expression, youth, children, pleasures, romance, financial speculation, sports, games, royalty, and nobility. This House is ruled by the playful, life-affirming Sun and imaginative Leo.
- The Sixth House: public health, personal health, charities, welfare, work methods, service industries, labor unions, civil and military service, and employees. This House is ruled by intellectual, informed Mercury and careful Virgo.

- The Seventh House: agents, international relations, business partnerships, legal affairs, contracts, politics, war, disputes, marriage, divorce, and public scandal. This House is ruled by tender, sophisticated Venus and connected by Libra.
- The Eighth House: corporations, taxes, financial dealings, insurance, debts, mortgages, communes, stock markets, death, rebirth, regeneration, renewal, the occult, and transformation of energy. This House is ruled by warlike Mars, with intense Scorpio and through a catalyst Pluto.
- The Ninth House: distant travels, foreign affairs, trade, the law, the courts, higher education, philosophy, church, and prophecy. This House is ruled by lucky Jupiter and metaphysical and academic Sagittarius.
- The Tenth House: honors, career rewards, fame, promotions, professional opportunities or status, the government, the executive and public life. This House is ruled by diligent, solemn Saturn and hard-working, intensive Capricorn.
- The Eleventh House: government finance, social programs, group co-operation, idealistic associations, theater, hope for the future, friends, and profitable inventions. This House is ruled by artistic and scientific Uranus, and peculiar Aquarius.
- The Twelfth House: dreams, intuition, instincts, karma, the subconscious mind, secrets, enemies, prisons, hospitals, monasteries, spirituality, exile, and searching for self-renewal. This House is ruled by mystical, selfless Neptune, and empathetic Pisces.

Planets

Each of the planets is used to coordinate with a zodiac sign and will influence some of the traits of that particular Sign:

- Sun: the planet of life, vitality, ego, creativity, and expression.
- Moon: linked to moods, emotions, femininity, intuition, mothers, and children.
- Mercury: full of logic, intellect, perception, thinking, and communication

- Venus: connected to romance, love, pleasure, femininity, beauty, and art.
- Mars: associated with power, aggression, drive, instincts, and masculinity.
- Jupiter: the planet of luck, religion, growth, abundance, expansion, higher learning, and travel.
- Saturn: linked with time, discipline, structure, restrictions, authority, and limitations.
- Uranus: connected to individualism, science, rebellion, revolution, eccentricity, humanitarianism, and inventions.
- Neptune: the planet of spirituality, dreams, illusion, delusions, oneness, and addictions.
- Pluto: associated with healing, transformation, alchemy, obsession, healing, life, and death.

Gemstones

- January – Capricorn – Garnet (from the Latin "granatum" which means seed); it resembles a pomegranate seed. This stone represents loyalty, trust, and friendship.
- February – Aquarius – Amethyst, as with other quartz crystals, this tone has frequently been linked to psychic abilities and can help the wearer gain spiritual focus and clarity.
- March – Pisces – both Aquamarine and Bloodstone can be linked to this month. Aquamarine is named because of its color ("aqua" meaning water). This has been associated with safe water voyages and protecting sailors. Aquamarine is also meant to produce a calming affect on the wearer. Bloodstone is connected with being both wise and brave.
- April – Aries – Diamond has long been linked to healing properties and it is believed that they can remove impurities and toxins from the wearer. Diamonds also represent innocence and purity.
- May – Taurus – Emerald which is connected to rebirth, luck, renewal, and youth.
- June – Gemini – both Pearl and Moonstone. Pearl is the only birthstone that is created naturally by a living organism and doesn't need to be polished. Pearl represents the sea and natural beauty. Moonstones are typically associated with their ability to metamorphose in appearance.
- July – Cancer – Ruby that is associated with wealth, wisdom, and love. Rubies are also used to awaken the senses and provide the wearer with a greater sense of self-awareness.
- August – Leo – Peridot with healing properties is said to ward off nightmares. It is also thought to bring the wearer great influence and power. Peridot is formed deep underground and are often brought to the surface by volcanoes.
- September – Virgo – Sapphire has been connected with protecting any wearer from harm and to bring about heavenly blessings.
- October – Libra – Opals which are a vibrant, radiant, colored stones representing versatility and diversity.
- November – Scorpio – Topaz and Citrine. Both of these stones are associated with wellness, healing, warmth, and energy.

- December – Sagittarius – Tanzanite and Turquoise. These stones are associated with protecting travelers from harm and keeping alive their taste for adventure.

Dates of the Cusps of a Sign

Zodiac cusps represent the days where one sign is rising as another sign sets. It is a propitious time to be born as these cusps are moments of surprise, concession, variation, beginnings, and endings. The cusps are set with new perspectives, possibilities and knowledge about the traits of these cusps can be truly illuminative.

- AQUARIUS/PISCES Cusp : February 16 - February 22 The Cusp of Sensitivity
    - Those on the cusp of Aquarius-Pisces are both procrastinators and goal-oriented. Although at times, their procrastination can be due to disorganization. This Sign has a lot of creative energy, emotion, and compassion, so they sometimes forget daily chores and organizing.
    - Ruled by both Uranus and Neptune, people under this Sign are very loved, brilliant, amazing, creative, and highly intelligent. Others may not "get" you, but you understand others. Your mind may work differently, but it does work beautifully.

- CAPRICORN/AQUARIUS Cusp: January 17 - January 22 The Cusp of Mystery & Imagination
    - For those born under the Capricorn-Aquarius cusp, their private life is very important to them, and they are very involved in their dreams and inner fantasies.
    - This cusp Sign might be disappointed with their real life. The dullness of reality can be constricting for the Capricorn-Aquarius. This may end up affecting relationships.
    - Capricorn-Aquarians are good at communication and their most satisfying relationships involve intellectual

and lively discussions. Although the pairing of Saturn and Uranus is creative and emotional and creative, they also admire logic and reasoning. Those under this Sign can be competitive and driven. However, combined with their creativity, this can make them a great success in work.
  - Those under this Cusp Sign have many contradictions in their personalities: they need security but love freedom; enjoy learning but can be overwhelmed by life's challenges; driven to improve and change the world, but disenchanted by reality.
  - Sometimes overly critical, it can alienate others.

- SAGITTARIUS/CAPRICORN Cusp : December 19 - December 25 The Cusp of Prophecy

  - People under this Cusp Sign have an uncanny sense of what is needed and are usually the ones who can deliver what is needed. This Sign is trustworthy, ambitious, and optimistic enough to make change happen.
  - With a meticulous personality, Sagittarius-Capricorn has a real knack for thorough preparation and makes for the perfect travel companion.
  - As part of a relationship, the Sagittarius-Capricorn can be a terrific partner who is dependable, loyal, and understanding. Unfortunately, they also have an intense desire to control their surroundings and may have a temper.

- SCORPIO/SAGITTARIUS Cusp : November 19 - November 24 The Cusp of Revolution

  - Scorpio has a dark and intense energy that might seem a little rebellious. But that should be expected from someone ruled by Jupiter, Mars, and Pluto.
  - Scorpio-Sagittarius learns by doing and is self-taught experts. This Sign can apply what they have learned to enjoy new adventures. This can then make them wonderful authority figures.
  - With the potential to be powerful and truly progressive, those under this sign need to maintain objectivity, not let

their emotions get the better of them, and keep knee-jerk reactions to a minimum.
- Jealousy can be a weakness so people under this Sign can be possessive in relationships, but they can also be romantic, kind, and loving.
- If you are a Scorpio-Sagittarius, seriously consider self-employment. And when it comes to your professional interactions, focus on generosity and kindness.
- Although pessimism and demeaning attitude may be a dominant trait, their lust for life will make you want to go with them anywhere.

- LIBRA/SCORPIO: October 19 - October 25 The Cusp of Drama & Criticism

    - The people under Libra-Scorpio cusp speak the truth, no matter whom it might hurt. This trait can be useful in both personal and professional areas, but can also cause some drama if it is not delivered constructively and might come across as bossy and sarcastic.
    - In relationships, the Libra-Scorpio cusp is loyal and romantic, but may have to be reminded that jealously will not improve the relationship.
    - Determination and tenacity are handy in the professional life of a Libra-Scorpio, which can give them what they need to achieve the goals they set for themselves.

- VIRGO/LIBRA Cusp : September 19 - September 24 The Cusp of Beauty

    - Like Libras, Virgo-Libra cusps can be obsessed with beauty. With the addition of a good eye for details, a Virgo-Libra can be the ultimate art lover.
    - People under this cusp sign are inclined to be creative, intelligent, super charismatic, sensitive, and kind. They are drawn to beautiful art, attractive people, and more sensual pleasures. Event planning and art curator are both great career choices for the Virgo-Libra cusp. But with this, they need to ensure they aren't just focused on the outside, superficial of those around them.

- With their sense of responsibility and fairness, they are always looking out for others using their nurturing tendencies. When involved in a relationship, they will always take care to ensure they are doing the little things that make their lover feel special.
- Some of a Virgo-Libra's strongest points are the open-mindedness and fairness they approach team project with. As long as both sides can approach it respectfully, they even enjoy a healthy debate occasionally as well.

- LEO/VIRGO Cusp : August 19 - August 25 The Cusp of Exposure

    - For those under this cusp, fire meets the earth, passion meets meticulousness, and command meets carefulness. These traits that seemingly don't match can make the Leo-Virgo feel in a constant state of conflict.
    - The conflict may be between the sides that are introverted and extroverted. Independence, secrecy, communication and leadership are all dominated traits and a challenge is to know what and when to say things. If a person under this cusp sign has a cause they are championing, they can be wonderfully persuasive. There is an activist at the heart of every one of them. And although they may enjoy the cause, their need for secrecy and privacy may be a stumbling block and may cause problems within a group.
    - Those under this cusp sign crave intimacy but it is something that they struggle with, especially the exposure that is required for true intimacy. This may seem to be an odd struggle when, half the time, those under this sign are direct, loud, and very communicative.

- CANCER/LEO Cusp : July 19 - July 25 The Cusp of Oscillation

    - Leo is fiery while Cancer is more emotional and when combined, can cause the smallest issues to blow out of proportion. And this makes for never a dull moment.
    - The Cancer-Leo cusp is centered on movement, both physical and emotional. Constantly in flux when it comes to emotions, they may struggle for balance and might

benefit from meditation or spirituality. Although seemingly shy at first, they will warm quickly and then may gravitate to the spotlight.
    - Those under this sign may be sensitive to criticism, so be careful on the wording of any suggestions. With an an excellent memory, they can also occasionally hold a grudge. But they love to be loved and make it a lot of fun to share a moment with. Unfortunately, they are also easily wounded with harsh words.

- GEMINI/CANCER Cusp : June 19 - June 24 The Cusp of Magic
    - Those under this sign often find themselves in the spotlight and the center of attention. But their outgoing personality may hide a collection of raw emotions, just under the surface. However, this makes them affectionate and sensitive.
    - Although they may seem easy to read, Gemini-Cancers are known to be private about their feelings. Friends and family may not even be aware of what's going on in their life, but they will have a thorough knowledge of the thoughts and feelings of everyone around them.
    - Once a Gemini-Cancer commits, they are in 100%, but this may take awhile. And they still may seem a little flirty, even after the commitment is made. Since they are ruled the Moon and Mercury, they want to surround themselves with people they trust. However, for this sign, trust is often hard to come by.
    - The family is valued and important to this cusp sign and that will include friends who act like family, blood relatives, and those that have made it to the inner circle.

- TAURUS/GEMINI Cusp : May 19 - May 24 The Cusp of Energy
    - The energy and charm of Gemini links with the diligent and tolerant Taurus. A very powerful cusp, combining modest and smart; adaptable and creative; and grounded and ambitious. But very productive, they can also spread themselves too thin at times. When you feel like you can do it all, it may be hard to say no to anyone who asks.

- o Great communicators, these people can talk to anyone about anything, but are not as skilled at listening, so they might monopolize a conversation and talking over their companions. This includes being sympathetic to friends who are going through the drama of their own and want to talk it through.
- o Independence and acknowledgment for hard work are important to those under this cusp. Represented by both Mercury and Venus, they contain a boundless energy when focused, making it a positive trait, but when undirected, may cause some anxiety.

- ARIES/TAURUS Cusp : April 19 - April 24 The Cusp of Power

    - o This cusp combines some of the most dominant personalities in the zodiac. Given any power, they will go straight to the top, and then some.
    - o The power is buffered by a generous spirit. Governed by Venus and Mars, those under this sign are typically nurturing friends, art lovers, and thoughtful leaders. "Work hard and play hard" is their motto, but this may be a tad bit overwhelming to themselves and those around them.
    - o As powerful leaders and problems solvers, the people under this cusp love to give advice. And if the advice has to do with getting a promotion or solving a difficult challenge, then definitely follow what they say. But, if you are asking about how to heal a broken heart or win back a lost love, then perhaps you are better off asking another. Aries-Taurus is not as tuned into emotions as they are in problem solving.

- PISCES/ARIES Cusp : March 19 - March 24 The Cusp of Rebirth

    - o A highly successful cusp, the Pisces-Aries make unconventional but effective leaders. They're not afraid to take action, but may over-think a situation which creates doubt in their mind. This may cause projects to

idle, and then their impulsiveness may take over. This can make any ride with them exciting and challenging.
- o Those under this cusp sign will push boundaries, and may not even be aware they are doing so. Occasionally, this can lead to misunderstandings or hurt feelings, but those born under the Pisces-Aries cusp can be very good at making others feel comfortable.
- o Ruled by Mar and Neptune, this cusp is very interested not only in their own success but are very gratified in helping close friends and family to achieve success as well. They are very good at achieving this success if they can keep their impatience under control and improve their communication abilities.

Greek/Roman Gods who represent the signs:

- Aries: the Greek god Ares (Roman god Mars), who is associated with war, bloodlust, violence, hate, courage, and civil order. Sacred animals for Ares are the alligator, vulture, dogs, and venomous snakes.
- Taurus: the Greek goddess Aphrodite (Roman god Venus), who is associated with love and beauty. The sacred animal for Aphrodite is the dove.
- Gemini: the Greek god Hermes (Roman god Mercury), who is linked to deception, thieves, travelers, medicine, trade, travel, messengers, cunning wiles, diplomacy, language, writing, athletics, and animal husbandry. Hermes was a messenger god who escorts souls of the dead to Hades. Sacred animals for Hermes are the ram, tortoise, and hawk.
- Cancer: Greek goddess Artemis (Roman goddess Diana) the virgin goddess of the hunt, hunting, virginity, childbirth, wilderness, wild animals, and plague. Sacred animals for Artemis are wild boars, deer, and bears.
- Leo: Greek god Apollo (Roman god Apollo), who is connected to prophecy, arts, music, light, music, healing, plagues, poetry, truth, archery, and the Sun. Sacred animals for Apollo are swans, dolphins, deer, ravens, cicadas, hawks, crows, cows, and snakes.

- Virgo: Greek god Hermes (Roman god Mercury) who is linked to medicine, deception, thieves, travelers, messengers, language, cunning, trade, wiles, writing, diplomacy, athletics, and animal husbandry. Mercury is the messenger god who leads souls of the dead to Hades. Sacred animals for Hermes are ram, hawk, and tortoise.
- Libra: Greek goddess Aphrodite (Roman goddess Venus) is the goddess of beauty and love. Sacred animal for Aphrodite is the dove.
- Scorpio: Greek god Hades (Roman god Pluto) who is the god of death, the underworld, and the hidden wealth of the Earth. Hades' sacred animal is an owl.
- Sagittarius: Greek god Zeus (Roman god Jupiter) who is the king of the Greek gods and oversees clouds, sky, power, air, weather, storms, thunder, law, fate, and order. According to Greek mythology, Zeus is the ruler of Mount Olympus. Zeus' sacred animals include the bull and the eagle.
- Capricorn: Greek god Chronos (Roman god Saturn) who is in charge of time. Chronos is the cruel and tempestuous force of chaos and disorder that gave birth to Zeus and all the other gods/goddesses.
- Aquarius: Greek god Uranus (Roman god Ouranos) who is associated with the sky and the original ruler of the universe.
- Pisces: Greek god Poseidon (Roman god Neptune) who is connected to storms, earthquakes, the sea, rivers, floods, droughts, and the creator of horses. Sacred animals include the dolphin and the horse.

Conclusion

Thank you for reading *Astrology*. Let's hope it was informative and able to provide you with all of the tools you need to achieve your goals for whatever they may be.

Remember, the best way to take Astrology is to focus on the positive and take advantage of the information about each sign in your life! Believe what you want to believe and remember life is in your hands and Astrology is there to help.

Finally, if you found this book useful in any way, Please leave a review on Amazon as it allows me to produce more quality books!

Enneagram

Modern Day Enneagram Discovery Of Yourself And Others Through Personality Types And Subtypes Guiding You Towards Purpose, Awareness, Self Knowledge And Healthy Relationships

Alex Fletcher

© Copyright 2018 - All rights reserved.

It is not legal to reproduce, duplicate, or transmit any part of this document in either electronic means or in printed format. Recording of this publication is strictly prohibited.

Table Of Contents

Introduction: A Guide to Spiritual Transformation.................. 127

Chapter 1: Three Structures, Wings Lines and Integration 134

Chapter Two: Personality Types 159

Chapter Three: Personality Type Test 171

Chapter Four: Subtypes (27) 181

Chapter Five: Self-Awareness And Growth Through Your Personality Type 190

Chapter Six: Enneagram and Relationships/Friendships 196

Conclusion.. 202

Introduction: A Guide to Spiritual Transformation

The enneagram is a powerful type of gateway towards the understanding of others and self-awareness. It gives a description of different dynamics and structures concerning the major personality types by creating a path to a life which is more integrated and rewarding. It comes from the Greek word 'ennea' which loosely translates to nine, and 'grammos' that entails a written symbol.

So these are nine distinct strategies for relating to the self and others. Each type for the enneagram represents a different thought approach that comes from a different inner motivation and perspective of the world. The enneagram enables a better understanding thus through universal language which transcends nationality, culture, religion and even gender.

Your enneagram core functions as a home base from which one can make sense of integration and individuation. It is crucial to keep in mind that different enneagrams can display similar behavior. The styles are not based solely according to behavior and outward representations can be deceiving.

In order to distinguish between the different enneagrams, one has to access motivation in order to explore the reasons why people may choose to act in a particular manner and why acting in this way is given value by that person.

History of the enneagram

The earliest references for the enneagram as historically documented would be in the sacred geometry of the Pythagoreans that were interested in the deeper meaning of numbers 4000 years ago. This is a line of mystical mathematics which then went to Plato and Plotinus. There are some that believe the tradition was then assimilated into esoteric Judaism through a Jewish Neo Platonist philosopher where it is represented as the tree of life in the symbolism that relates to the nine folds. There are other variations of the symbol that can be seen in Islamic Sufi traditions also.

During the 1300s, the Naqshbandi order of Sufism which was the 'brotherhood of the bees', allegedly preserved and passed on the enneagram traditions. After that, it is said that it found its way into esoteric Christianity through Pseudo Dionysius and via Ramon Lull. More concrete understanding concerning the enneagram in recent history is from George Gurdjieff, a Russian teacher of esoteric knowledge who was a contemporary of Freud. Gurdjieff considered the enneagram as having the key to all knowledge which lay in the universe. He used the enneagram to explain the laws concerning creation and implies how he got to know about the enneagram in the 20s during his visit to the Sufi Sarmouni monastery, in Afghanistan.

In another part of the world, the enneagram teachings sprung up through Oscar Ichazo as part of the Africa Training in South America. The enneagram was apparently found to organize the different laws operating in the human person. While Gurdjieff used the process of the enneagram for all reality including the human individual, Ichazo made better use of the figure and dynamics for explaining the functioning of the human psyche. Another psychologist, Claudio Naranjo took up from where Ichazo left off and brought the enneagram further into western psychology during the 90s by framing the concepts into contemporary psychological language.

An evaluation concerning the origins of the enneagram and its teachings is defined in terms of the characteristic limitations of particular personality modes. The issue from that redefinition derives from the part that according to the enneagram teaching every individual has to choose a personality type as the basic strategy for coping with the environment that you may be in at the moment. All personality types happen to have their intrinsic motivations as sinning becomes inevitable apparent. If sin is inevitable as it is resultant from one personality type, that would mean the solution to sin is found in the compensation of ones personality through following the prescriptions given by the enneagram. The remedy of sinning becomes a matter of great knowledge as opposed to reformation of the will. In Christianity, the sin is an unhealthy behavior and can be countered through improved understanding as it is a moral problem at the roots before God. The teachings given by the enneagram obscures the Christian understanding when it comes to sin because the origins are pagan.

There are a number of theoretical papers which have tried to develop potential applications for the enneagram. In business, the enneagram has been integrated into a theoretical paper that presents new frameworks for the acquisition of knowledge which proposes that the enneagram be utilized in order to develop and integrate knowledge within the social sciences. There was a paper on market segmentation that came up with the suggestion of utilizing enneagram typology in order to initiate marketing strategies for the market segments in the region done by Kamieni in 2005. The suggestions for improving spirituality in the work environment recommended the introduction of the enneagram as means for the corporations to create a company which was more harmonious and profitable.

Why it's true

The enneagram tradition defines personality as the lifetime accumulation for the emotional and mental patterns that constitute the persona. This being the individual that believes themselves to be and the way they are presented to the world.

These patterns may include the habitual ways of thought, perceptions and feelings. The words such as ego, personality and false sense of self are similar and used very interchangeably with the teachings that are propagated through the enneagram. The personality is claimed to be an imitation of the true self. It is fixated and reacts to the outer environment which is changing all the time with predictable and conditioned reactions. That being said, it is possible to claim the personality that we have gotten used to, as opposed to who we really are. The real being or the true self could be considered as a process rather than the fixed identity. Essence flows are changeable and they respond fresh and appropriately considering the altering situations of the outer environment.

Determination of an individual's personality type with the use of the enneagram system does not necessarily put one inside a defined box of nine archetypes. It assists people to see the box from where they are able to experience the world. With this in mind, one can step outside their worldview. Ideally speaking, personality is effective in allowing one to express themselves because they are able to categorize and identify who they really are. At the same time there can be issues when people get stuck in automatic habits. In discovering these unconscious patterns, people are able to lead lives which are more fulfilling and enjoy relationships which are overall healthier. Working within the enneagram model allows people to become successful in their relationships at home and within the working environment. Through understanding automatic reactions and blind spots, people can become more flexible with others in their lives and understand what others are feeling and thinking. This making it easier to tolerate other and be more compassionate. It also helps people to not take the negative reactions or their hostility in such a manner that it is personal. Through the identification of how you are emotionally and psychologically defensive, the enneagram allow you to have a chance at profound growth. At another level it also allows you to develop your relationship with yourself and better this, so that you can become more productive towards yourself and anything within your life.

Simply, the enneagram enables and grows ones capacity when it comes to self-observation. It provides vision for how the healthiest manifestation of people's types can look. Using this detail, it sets a path for the manner in getting to a higher level of awareness. Each type within the enneagram has particular behaviors that satisfy its needs and desires. This is the main strategy of the particular type in life. That would be driving much of what the type does. The enneagram is able to help people spot when they are being run by their passions, allowing people to satisfy their needs in a healthier manner.

For example, the passion for type seven happens to be gluttony. This is the traditional meaning for overeating which extends to over consumption. The people with this type look for experiences in trying to find a sense of fulfillment which they fear may remain elusive. In truth, they may feel that nothing they embark on will bring the fulfillment which they look for to bring happiness and contentment.

Enneagram as a self-discovery tool to benefit your life

The enneagram allows for one to get on a journey towards self-enlightenment and acceptance for who you are. Everyone has a basic driving force and a preferred strategy set for unique talents and strengths that make us individuals. We look at the world and the present era with specific perspectives and we are drawn in particular directions as individuals. These preferences can harden into modes of behavior, which also strangle the ways in which we grow. At times when people first discover the particular type they are, they might say that they would like to change to another type. That is an indication they are judging one type to be more desirable as compared to another. The key to utilizing the enneagram would be exploration without the use of judgment. The question is if each pattern provided a large reservoir of talent, which is equally valuable. You are undoubtedly growing and maturing everyday so there should not be a limit to the potentials irrespective of your type. Every evidence points to the fact that no enneagram type is better than the other. In each archetype there are different levels of maturity and generativity. The level of maturity may vary though in different contexts.

Each type of enneagram represents a deep habit. It shows a theme that for a lot of people is constant throughout their life, though the possibilities for the mental, physical or spiritual developments have no bounds. The type is a fundamental form of human habit. With some technology and coaching, it is possible to utilize the information gained from this information to transform patterns for more effective behavior and perspectives.

As we study our types, it begins to dawn on us that there is a range of healthy to unhealthy behaviors we engage in unwittingly. When we are relaxed, we may feel safe and have natural gifts that are inherent to our type that are at our disposal. Similarly, when under stress, we have ways of reacting that may run contrary to the best intentions we have. When triggered we may also react in the best way to protect ourselves from pain, fear or shame and respond so quickly that we do not even acknowledge the effect that it has on other people. When growing to understand our type, we develop the right skills which are particular to that type and that may allow us to reduce the levels of stress we harbor through reactivity and our quick responses which negatively affect the ones that are around us. This also allows the illustration of the greatest gifts and as we continue to learn, there is an understanding that others also have unconscious patterns and reactions which are predictable during times of crises, happening beyond the level of present awareness.

With more study, one may start to develop valuable traits such as compassion and understanding for themselves and others concerning the patterns of the type and then grow to appreciate just how fast any one can be triggered and how much it is not possible to note the patterns. Over the course of time it becomes easier to develop skills that would slow things down and bring us out of the trance that instilled patterns we engage. We can then become compassionate and sensitive to the emotional vulnerabilities of everyone and become skilled at holding space for them. Under stress, each category has a way they disconnect from their loved ones emotionally.

In depth exploration concerning the enneagram also assists one to navigate their relationships with more skill. Knowing the types of your family and colleagues can increase your understanding on their fears, defenses and motivations, allowing you to understand how they would interact with you and others. The other reason you should take this journey into self-exploration is the commitment to living a conscious and caring life though every day you may come across situations and people that could result in self-sabotaging reactions. Even if you had been on a spiritual path for some time, you may still be humbled by the manner that the unconscious reactions bring you to patterns that you had thought had been outgrown.

It could be that you tend to space when your spouse expresses painful emotions because it disrupts your carefree attitude, or you may turn to alcohol or other drugs when you feel like you are being shunned or things are not going your way. Irrespective of the pattern, everyone comes with habits that block self-expression and joy. All of these patterns which are negative cause their own suffering and they are linked to habits of the different enneagram types. Even in the event that you can recite deep spiritual truths when these patterns are triggered, you may still forget the bigger picture of who you are and the unique gifts that you can share with the world. The question then arises on how one can find clarity and free themselves from the fears, motivations and desires that fuel behavioral patterns and trigger other reactions from others.

Chapter 1: Three Structures, Wings Lines and Integration

Three centers

Human beings have three major ways of how they experience the world and that would be through thinking, feeling and sensation. The enneagram model and other mystical approaches considers three centers of intelligence along with perception of which mediate the life experiences that people have and their reactions to them. This corresponding to the heart, head and the body. From a psychological point of view, everyone utilizes the three centers. Everyone senses the environment and has an emotional reaction to it or thinks about things though each type may favor one of them as the main channel for the perception and response to incidences. The diagram then differentiates into three triads, which all correspond to one of the centers and the types within that are referred to as the head, heart and the body types. Each particular center has its own way of experiencing life and the negative emotion and concerns that are linked. The main types within each tried would be the ones that favor the particular center and reveal ways of dealing with that issue.

The nine-enneagram modes have been grouped into three centers, which include the heart, head and the body. While everyone has three centers, the personality type has a particular strength and a home base in one of them. The body center is inclusive of type 8, 9 and 1 which is formed as a response to anger. The head center has types 5, 6 and 7 that are created as a response to fear or anxiety and the heart center has types 3, 2 and 4 which is formed as a response to shame and a self-image formed. Understanding of One's primary center provides a significant key towards the development of personal and professional potential by overcoming the blind spots.

The three centers within a person interact with each other and one cannot work on one center without actually affecting the other two. As a matter of fact the center, which the enneagram type resides, is the psyche that people are least able to function freely as the function has been blocked by the ego. For example, the enneagram type nine, which is the body center, is the enneagram type which is mostly disengaged with the body, not physically speaking but internally.

Considering there are many sets of three in the enneagram of personality, there are also several ways in which to unpack the whole enneagram in bite size chunks of three. It may take some time to absorb some of the complex data and you might not get it incorporated on the first try. That is part of its charm as the enneagram is always new and surprising, concerning its nuances of insight upon insight, which proceed to evolve over the course of time. If you use the enneagram for the purposes of just becoming a number and to forgive and explain bad habits, then that is missing the point. The point would be to utilize the enneagram as the platform for self-discovery and personal growth. After decades of study and witnessing, the enneagram will enable you to unveil your innermost self and secrets.

The body center

This center houses types 8, 9 and 1 as mentioned before and these have distortions in their instincts, the root of life force and vitality. The body center entails intelligence of the body, which is a direct experience of our existence. That being a sense of life, connecting with yourself and having communication with other things. When you are not present, you lose your sense of confidence, existing and fullness. The major emotion for the body center would be anger. This usually comes from an instinctual response pertaining to the sense of interference or being messed with. The unconscious fear is concerning unity and this is where people may lose themselves, their functioning or not being intact. The body center needs autonomy and it is concerned about the influence on the surroundings.

As such, a type 8 may tend to act out their anger or express it very easily or in a rapid manner. They may also place their guard up very quickly in such a manner that no one can get to them or hurt their feelings. Their anger can come from a number of situations where they or another individual experiences injustice.

The head center

This is where the thinking takes place as well as analysis, remembrance and the projection of ideas about what other people and events ought to be. The head based types include 5, 6 and 7 and they may respond to existence through the use of their thoughts. They may also have vivid imaginations and there is a strong ability to correlate and analyze ideas. Even those who are very gregarious claim they are very satisfied with the company that is brought by their own thoughts. For those types, thinking represents a way for the pre-empting of fear.

The mind has to keep all of its defenses and come up with a dissociated sense of yourself and produce a sense of direction. The main emotion when it comes to the head center would be fear. When you can experience the presence and stillness in a direct manner, you experience it as the ground of everything. That knowledge is the basis of faith. When you lose the ground of support and guidance, you may become panicky and fearful. The head center type needs security and they're concerned with beliefs and strategy. A type 5 may react to fear through retreating to their mind and so reducing personal needs. There is a need for example to master something in order to feel safe and to observe surroundings in order to make an analysis concerning what is going on. The type 6s respond to fear as well through considering what may happen in the worst case scenario. Usually, they could be ready for anything that may go wrong. They can look for guidance from those who are in charge in order to deal with no guidance issues or they can rebel against the said authorities when they become dependent. The type 7s as well react to fear through trying to turn awkward or uncomfortable situations into something which is exciting and new in order to avoid the feelings of fear. They may fear being trapped in pain, grief or anxiety and go into an activity that helps them escape or keeps them otherwise occupied.

The heart center

This is the place where people experience emotions or the sensations that tell people the way they feel as opposed to what they think about something. Emotions of the heart can range from the dramatic and the wrong to the most subtle or mute feelings. People overall feel connected to other people within this center but also have a yearning for fulfillment and love. They include the types 2, 3 and 4 these groups have distortions concerning their feelings. The heart is aware of the truth and it lets us know things such as identity and the truth of who we are. It is also where people derive a sense of meaning and glory about their existence. When a person says something that is resonating and true, the heart will be in agreement and you might feel connected to the message and to the person. As such, being in touch with the heart shows the quality of existence and shows how to know the truth. Another common emotion when it comes to the heart center would be shame. The types 2, 3 and 4 are in search for recognition, validation and mirroring. This is needed because when you are young, there is a limited capacity for self-reflection. You can only ascertain who you are through the perspectives of others. As such, when you do not get the attention that you would like there is some shame, deficiency and a sense of emptiness. The head centers want a lot of attention and are concerned with the way they are portrayed or their self-image.

The type twos can be caring for others in order to get good rapport and so they do not feel a sense of shame. They can create an image of being needed or likeable, though they have issues knowing what they need or feel. They often know this when there are a lot of people that are dependent on them for survival. Type Threes are very out of touch with their inner selves and believe they need positive feedback and affirmations from other people. They can find value and self-worth through performance in order to avoid the feelings of shame that could come about. They also try and project images of success into the community and look for the admiration of others in order to fuel their self-image.

The type fours may usually look for the reasons why they are unique when compared to other people. They initiate and sustain moods and use emotions as a means through which they can defend against being rejected. This is done through the dramatization of their hurts and losses, causing them to avoid deeper feelings and get attention or pity from other people. As such, the type twos externalize shame and create images of a great individual, the type threes feel conflict considering they have a lot of shame and cover this with an image of success. The type fours manage to internalize their shame and have initiated an image which illustrates their identity.

How the Enneagram centers work

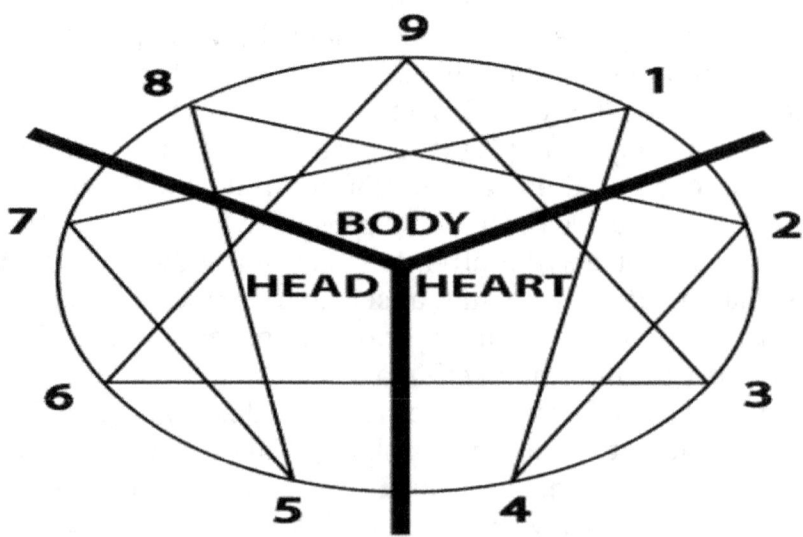

Source: http://enneagramphilosophy.tumblr.com/post/51066726963/enneagram-triads-1-primary-centres

A lot can be said concerning the way personality develops in the Enneagram. Each type may favor one center though everyone contains and is affected by the heart, head and the body centers within themselves in different ways. The enneagram is descriptive concerning different qualities of the centers for all human beings, which is a structure that is common to everyone, this then illustrating how this manifests differently for the various modes. There are 'two of us' inside all, which is the essential self-known and the personality that believes itself to be that of the individual. Of the two selves, the personality tends to manifest through habitual narrow modes of thought and survival reactions. These are referred to as passion, fixation and instinctual subtypes and they are the source of repetition within our daily lives. Describing of the essential self, heart and the head allows for a holy opposite which is a particular aspect of essence. These are known as the holy virtue and holy idea. The idea of virtue and the holy idea are more like holy seeds as opposed to holy opposites, considering they are with everyone at birth and name the divine qualities of the soul. People just forgot this as they learnt to deal with the world and developed personality defense structures. The personality masks and protects the essential self and it also does an imitation like a mirror that is reflecting back to front through looking for the forgotten aspects in the outside world instead of within. This would be the basis of differences between the nine types. In summary; one of the underlying structures for the types is that they have nine distinct ways of manifestation. For each of the nine, their spiritual qualities and psychological self seem to narrow their focus towards the attention of trying to imitate the innate forgotten qualities within their type.

The head center: fixation and holy idea

The fixation would be an indication of the personality's habitual pre-occupation or the focus of their attention. It may be described as the metaphorical hamster in the mental wheel. The holy idea on the other hand shows a state of awareness which is experienced rather than thought of by the spiritual head center at the time that it is free of the fixation.

The heart center: passion and holy virtue

The habitual underlying emotion of the heart center is known as Passion. Early Christians had known this aspect being one of the nine interruptions to the life of prayer as stated by Evagrius Ponticus. At the present, they correspond to the seven deadly sins added to fear and deceit. The essential state of being experienced in the heart is known as Holy Virtue, otherwise referred to as the virtue of essence.

The body center

The word subtypes means three survival instincts which are connected to the body center for the enneagram. Survival, which is the matter of life and death, is considered in the last resort through unconscious gut reaction and instinct. The nine fixations and passions define the personality attributes and they can be recognized as 'what a person does'. The subtypes define three different means of manifesting each type, this causing the behavior from them to be believed as a matter of life or death.

These instincts concern survival in fundamental areas such as:
1. Self-preservation, which is the right to exist with the energy focusing on material wellbeing.
2. There is a social consideration of the right to belong since human beings are tribal people. Survival is dependent on acceptance within the tribe.
3. There are sexual needs as everyone has the right to be loved. This is also related to the instinct to survive through what is newly created in one on one relationships irrespective of whether that is a baby or validation by another person.

Everyone tends to focus on one of these, depending on their experience towards the greatest threat to their essential self as they grew up. This includes whether people were fed, were warm, nurtured well, accepted by the family and their attempts to attract unconditional love. At the present there is some debate as whether the subtype focus is present from the time of birth, regardless of whether it is developmental and a result of the environment or a combination of the two just in the same way as an individual's adult persona is. In either case the result is while all three centers are important for happy functioning in life, one of them is going to be seen unconsciously as the greatest source of pain or threat. This then draws a lot of energy and attention to it and looks to be one of the greatest sources of happiness and satisfaction.

How the enneagram works

The enneagram is a tool for great subtlety though the central is based upon what happens to be quite simplistic. That is that the personality was developed in order to protect our higher self and is linked inseparably to it. There is a simple observation which allows the use of this knowledge and it is not unique to the Enneagram. We are consistent of two people. The first is the soul or the essence. It is neither thought, feeling or sensation yet it's the person. The other is the personality that identifies itself with thoughts, feelings and sensations. Most of the time, it is confused for the true self but it can be changed.

The difference between the spiritual and psychological nature is only just apparent. Both of them are integral to the people that we are. While being alive, there is a need for a personality in order to mediate between the higher selves and the world in order to assist in getting things done but there is also a need to recognize its nature. The personality represents a set of tools which help us through life while other parts do not assist very much. Though you might have adopted them in order to keep you safe, by the time you become an adult, they become part of the negative problems.

In order to change or transcend, the first thing that one has to know is what the problem is. If you want to make a journey it would be first helpful to create the journey as it helps in having a map of the terrain to know where you are on the map and what obstacles that you may come across. This is a big part towards the value of the Enneagram. It represents a map of the particular terrain. In the same manner that traversing the Sahara would not require one to pack snow climate gear, if your go-to habit is fear, then it will not help to work on anger and pride. Envy is a big issue for some people while anger is for others and so forth.

When it comes to essence, the higher self, and the mystical arts describe the attributes of the soul. The spiritual gifts and the essence of each of the nine types of the enneagrams are variations of being, consciousness and bliss. When you get presence, then you find that all three centers are united and the three gifts avail themselves.

The head center for one corresponds to the visualization center allegedly used in Buddhist meditations and a number of the practices that relate to Ignatian spirituality. The head center knows what is real and trusts it. That is to say that Christianity is trustworthy. This then relates to faith as it needs no proof because it only knows what is true and discerns the significance of what is in the unique time. This discernment lets us perceive the way that the world works and gives us wisdom in order to act in a courageous manner in harmony with the requirements of the world.

The head is the spiritual heart center opened in the Sufi and Christian practices. The liturgy, devotional prayer and changing all provided access to the spiritual heart. In the west, the heart is associated with love while in the enneagram; the concept of love which is unconditional belongs to the belly. This is a given and it is where people come from or who they are and where they return. The yearning for what is known as love is actually an outward movement for the soil and the urge to unite. The heart types know that it is about the relationships and the unfolding time and space because of the interweaving. The heart wants to reach out and respond and create something new when it comes to hope. The belly center finally has almost been forgotten in the west as an organ of spiritual perceptions. It is correspondent to the concept that is known as hara in Japan and is the focus of all practices that are rooted in Zen. Love exists as a necessary part for creation. The gifts of the belly center would have to do with the nature of reality of being and of presence.

According to Gurdieff, it is possible to identify the chief features as most of the work has been accomplished and the Enneagram allows for this to happen. The inner self differentiates between essence and personality and that would be the key towards spiritual growth. Through the means of self-observation it is possible to recognize the automatic reactions of the personality and then use them as the reminders for the qualities that we have. In that way, it then becomes possible to regain the ability to respond to life from a perspective which is not biased and in tune with the true self. If you are skilled, then the inner self may assist in realizing patterns and bring out the unused and hidden potentials. Knowledge of particular terrain makes the efforts that much easier and accurate. It is not a query for transcending or subduing the personality, but rather befriending it and learning the manner that it points us to. Irrespective of whether people approach the personal growth as spiritual or both, it's completely up to them. People are able to understand their background influences or mediate for long periods of time every day. Unless it increases the humane-ness and loving kindness and unless daily actions and thoughts are harmonious and creative, then it is not growth.

Wings lines and integration

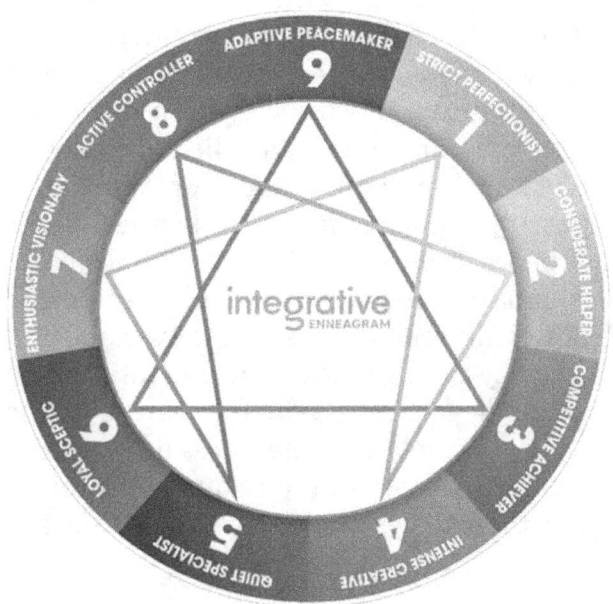

The enneagram is more than the nine types or points as represented on an intersection of a triangle. It is one of the psychodynamic frameworks which gives a strong model for understanding the manner in which integration and development work. It does not necessarily give a quick fix with a limited lifespan once there is insight. It allows individuals to develop themselves over the course of time as it proceeds to speak to us and the circumstances that continue to change. In the framework though, instincts, wings and the levels of integration are representative of the movement and journey that we are following in life.

The wings concern adjacent types to the core type on the enneagram circle. These neighbors may influence but they do not alter the core type. If the core type is like ice cream, then the wing would indicate the sauce that you can add to your ice cream, so to speak. That is not a second type of ice cream that you can add to the ice cream, it is just the flavor of the adjacent type. Everyone has access to both of their winds and each has a different set of resources and attributes that can be helpful at different times. Sometimes one of these wings proves to be more predominant and familiar. Some individuals do not like to add too much sauce to the wings, metaphorically speaking, while others like to balance it out. The wings are there to enable people to understand the types not in isolation but via their relationship to each other. Considering the types of the enneagram are viewed as a continuum, one's wings can assist with understanding the subtleties of one's core type. Through leaning into your wings from one side or the other, it becomes possible to expand your perspective and increase emotional and behavioral repertoires. The wings could also give a way to understand tensions and the effects on a person when they are stuck and then initiate the potential to reframe the situation as a point at which they can be able to develop into something more.

The gift of the enneagram is when it comes to potential and movement that flexes between the core, line of release and the apparent connection. There is an obvious question for those who are acquainting themselves with the enneagram as to whether people are just one type or a combination of two or more. The appropriate response is both yes and no obviously.

The enneagram is a dynamic framework, which is to state that it isn't restricted to one place on the figure. Individuals move around to the next enneagram which focuses on relying upon their necessities and specific conditions. While the fundamental personality remains the command post, we also invest some energy occupying or visiting a portion of the other personality types. This is definitely not an irregular procedure. The enneagram figure is demonstrative of the examples that every one of the personality types follow. Since the image is somewhat striking, when individuals originally go over the enneagram they may think about whether the lines imply anything. They are significant as the lines follow the courses that you travel when you experience distinctive moves in mindfulness and conduct in your day by day presence. You go along these lines from one point to the next and now and again you may return, moving forward at a quicker rate, barely seeing the move with regards to the viewpoint. On different occasions, you may have a more sensational move or even invest some energy in a point instead of the basic personality type.

It would appear there is some inalienable association of knowledge inside the chart. In this way, the enneagram is unique in relation to the next personality modes. There are different frameworks which offer a depiction of four or even sixteen types. However, the enneagram is something other than a basic rundown. It is an all-encompassing thing that is based by the arithmetic and symmetry of this graph returning a large number of years. With regards to people, however, the lines convey vital data concerning mental examples. Pieces of the lessons concerning the enneagram is somewhat mysterious. You may ask how the lines inside the graph can work as an indicator for the conduct of others in day by day life. There is by all accounts zero logical confirmation that all things are considered. The answer can be learnt through testing the hypothesis and checking whether it has down to earth esteem. One may have the capacity to see in your life certain examples as given by the lines which are in the chart. Seeing that it has been utilized by thousands amid the ages, there is by all accounts somewhat of an accord that these lines mean something or they allude to something which is unmistakable.

Lines of the diagram

▶ Arrow line points to disintegration
— Non-arrow line points to integration

There is a body inside the training that has customarily used the graph as a means for understanding the standards administering the universe like the events of phenomena and how they move in designs. The investigation was based by the properties of numbers and the usage of instinct as it started before the logical revelations of the ongoing occasions. Inside the cutting edge period, the examples of vitality might be evaluated or considered in manners which are more exact. However a few ideas including quantum material science conflict with the breaking points of the examinations as of now. There might be a lot of meta designs which have not been evaluated up until now also.

Amid the prior occasions, masterminds and researchers have taken a stab at clarifying the characteristic world utilizing graphs and numbers like the enneagram. While there is no featuring of that use of the enneagram in the present discourse about personality, there are a couple of numerical components that can help in the investigation of individuals.

When you take a gander at the nine pointed graph, it will end up obvious, there are covering sets of lines. One of them would be the triangle joining the points 3, 6 and 9. This internal triangle demonstrates the law of three that is there in both mainstream and religious settings. In the Christian religion, there are ideas that identify with the quantity of three, for example, the trinity of God, the Son and the Holy Spirit. In the mainstream world, the law of three can be depicted as the postulation, absolute opposite and the union. As indicated by the cutting edge father of the enneagram Gurdjieff, who conveyed the enneagram to the west in 1915 and presented the idea in this way. Point three would be the place for the commencement of vitality. Point three is noted as the place of opposing and the improvement of vitality or blessed denying while point nine would be the place of interceding and the harmonization of vitality. The interesting thing concerning this issue is that the personality types that are related with these points hope to encapsulate something concerning these traits. Threes have a starting and going ahead component. The points sixes for the most part consider it for quite a while and consider advancement of the thought further to get the wrinkles out and to think of a refined arrangement. Nines are professedly individuals that look for equalization and concordance. They are the individuals who are mediators. You can now and again portray personality types 3, 6 and 9 as displaying the characteristics for no, perhaps and yes. The lines inside the internal triangle interface the personality types. In the following area, the content will consider the manner in which they move forward and backward from a point to another amid various occasions.

Regardless, there is something, which is very valuable about the possibility of threes. Keeping in mind the end goal to start another venture, there is the requirement for enough inspiration and starting vitality. In spite of the fact that to an extent we know things generally don't go ahead in a straight line and instead appears in work for personal development. There is obstruction all the time regarding something in ourselves or the condition that should be countered. If you can draw in this arrangement of deterrents in a way which is wise to see it as a helpful piece of the procedure, the first arrangement or the aim advances into something that is significantly more fruitful. The other method to see this on the off chance that you can have a decent discussion or gainful clash between the starting parts and the opposing parts is you move to some goals or amalgamation. In spite of the fact that without that procedure, activities or people would not form or develop into something which is better. The other arrangement of the lines inside the enneagram would be the one associating the points 4, 2, 1, 8, 5, 7. This can be used so as to show the law of seven which is a number set that is connected with the seven notes in the regular melodic scale. While the law of three concerns the characteristics of vitality or three types of power at work, the law of seven concerns the movement for vitality and the movements of steps towards each task or action. There are individuals that have observed the law of seven to be very helpful in the arranging of their exercises to ensure a specific end goal. As of now, it is just conceivable to see how this arrangement of lines and the connections between the numbers inside the set advise the investigation of the personality types. In the event that you happen to separate 1 by the number 7 you then get something which is repeating from the decimal.. The hypothesis of the enneagram proposes that personality types inside the numbers 1, 4, 2, 8, 5 and 7 tend to move forward and backward thusly relying upon some interior conditions.

Wing points and dynamic points of movement

There are two methods of movement that exist on the enneagram. Every one of them has distinctive characteristics in this way. One of them concerns the movement around the periphery of the hover points delineated on each side of the personality type. The adjacent points as specified before are the wing points. The other is the movement inside the enneagram to the two points that are associated with one's point by the straight lines. These are what are alluded to as the 'Dynamic Points'. These points are the nearby neighbors and one can visit them since they are ideally adjacent. It doesn't take a considerable measure to move and embrace a viewpoint and the personal perspective of the wing points. In spite of the fact that they are distinctive modes from your own particular, you can undoubtedly see the world through their eyes or go up against their conduct either positively or negatively. At the point when people are finding their sort, they may relate to some wing points. Truly, a few people could see themselves similarly with the two neighboring types. However they may not know which one is the essential kind.

It may be the case that the purpose behind this is each type can be portrayed as a mix of the two wing points. For one, in the event that you happen to mix a nine alongside a two then you may think of what has all the earmarks of being a one. Additionally, on the off chance that you mix a four and a six then you may think of a five. Individuals approach both of their wings. Every one of them has an alternate arrangement of assets and characteristics which might be used as a portion of the time. In say this there is proof that one of these wings is transcendent or a commonplace. One may watch themselves with a specific end goal to find that they have a prevalent wing, or you may encounter moving to the two wings on an equivalent premise. In any examples that hold, it is clear the fundamental personality type can be influenced by the nearness of the wings which at that point prompts noteworthy fluctuations in conduct and viewpoint among the nine classes.

As opposed to moving to the wing points, the movement inside the enneagram isn't that simple and can be a critical move in the experience of our lives. They are named as psychodynamic or even dynamic considering the personality experiences noteworthy changes. You may likewise be in an alternate point of view and style of conduct. You and other people who are a major part of your life will come to know about these progressions. There are times these movements are befuddling and irritating just as they were occurring outside of a man's control. In spite of the fact when mindful of these movements, you can oversee them sufficiently and they can be productive for personal and expert advancements. It seems as though you approach another arrangement of assets and it is a set which includes esteem or makes the expected equalization to the standard personality type. The movement of these dynamic points can help with venturing out of the limits and extending the choices sufficiently. It additionally implies to not getting stuck inside the habitual style of response to the environment. Whether you are on the inner triangle or on another set of lines, there may be two lines which connect the personality type to two other points. However, each line presents a different quality and direction to it. In one of the directions, such as the forward directions, there is the resource point. This is the point where you can access a quality which would provide some assistance to taking action in the world. There are a number of enneagram teachers that name this as the stress point considering whether you go there and when you're under a significant amount of stress, accessing the competencies and intelligences of this point. Both claims are true though the stress point has a negative type of connotation that you are using the term 'the resource point'. This is not necessarily a negative thing though it can be a bit uncomfortable.

In the other direction, moving backwards provides the relaxation or the heart point. When you go towards that direction, you move to inhabit personality modes which are considered to be valuable for transformation and personal growth. That point is key to a number of the underlying issues within the personality of an individual as the undeveloped side of the self. It is as if you have to relax and let down the normal defenses of the normal way of seeing the world to become flexible as well as vulnerable to others and situations. When you feel safe and secure, you can then go deeper within yourself to learn more about who you are and become available to loved ones. Obviously coming to terms with some of these core issues and feelings within the relaxation point may be a bit challenging. There is a propensity for one to snap to their usual personal type and its perspective and standard practices. On the other hand, if you have the ability to stay long enough within the relaxation point to integrate various lessons then there is a possibility to re-inhabit the personality type with more balance and integration.

As such in the enneagram, you move toward the resource point which in this manner; 3 would go to 9 then 6 then 3 and so on. It may also go to the other set of lines where 1 goes to 4 then 2 then 8 then 5 then 7 then 1. Going to the relaxation point means backwards within the opposite direction. That would then become clearer as you go through the personality types as provided within the book.

Point One: Wing points

At the point when the ninth wing is predominant, the Ones are more arranged toward amicability and equalization. That involves the drive to get things right which is intervened by a longing to be agreeable. They would then be able to end up quieter and go at a slower pace. A potential drawback to these wings is it can make the Ones set in their ways which is less versatile or adaptable to the desires for different people or the requirements for the occasion. One preferred standpoint to this wing is the way to be beneficial inside a methodological or relentless way, while keeping consideration to rightness and quality.

At the point when the wing is predominant, the Ones are drawn toward associations with different people. Doing the correct things at the present implies additionally being strong and supportive. With this wing being dynamic, the Ones are more expressive and ground breaking. A potential drawback here would be nervousness or being vexed which originates from interpersonal clashes or the feeling that other individuals are not getting things done in the correct way. One favorable position to the wing is it would make it potentially viable as a blend for individuals association aptitudes. The assignment for the production of request and the correct outcomes would be centered more around the general population, instead of the material items.

Dynamic Points

The unwinding point for the Ones would be point Seven. Instead of looking to locate the one right away, the Ones may open up to new potential outcomes. It is less demanding for one to endure numerous plans and choices. They happen to be less incredulous of themselves and other individuals. At the point when the Ones begin to unwind into Seven, they can begin to shed a portion of the physical pressure so it is less demanding for them to have a great time and simply run with things. On the off chance that the unwinding point isn't incorporated in the correct way, it is conceivable that Ones can 'carry on' if the typical poise isn't there. They could result to eating or drinking too much. Despite the fact that when they prevail in the combination of the two points, there could be some enthusiasm and positive feeling of Seven which implants the obligation and diligent work of the One. Spontaneity and flexibility are acclimatized with intentionality and uprightness.

The resource point for Ones would be point four. This is normally where they would connect with being disturbed. The weakness however is there is a sentiment of stress in tough situations this creating emotions that may turn out as being excessively disordered or even forceful.

Point Two: Wing points

The way that the twos express themselves is balanced through an innate feeling to do things the right way. On the advantageous side, they happen to be more reserved and so they control themselves in ways where they show off their skills. They also happen to be thoughtful and balance aspects of self-control with the levels of their emotions to come out with a better assessment of scenarios. The bad thing with this combination of attributes is it can result in duality of natures which then leads to physical tension. They can become uncomfortable if they become too self-critical if everything has to be in its order. Self-containment that is with the One wing and the warmth and outgoing of Two initiates outgoing energy of Two which leads to stability and relative effectiveness.

When Three wing is predominant, then the Two might utilize their skill in order to consider the requirements of others in order to become more successful in their professions. They are very responsive. To a particular point, they are able to match Threes in every detail when it comes to working toward the objective. However, they are not Threes and over the course of time, they are going to have to slow things down. When the Three wing is active, the Two will make good performers. On the other hand, that particular wing point will make things harder over time to bring their attention to their needs, doubts and personal agendas.

Dynamic point

The Two then moves to the point four which is the place of relaxation and calm. As opposed to the usual paying attention to others to initiate a sense of security, at this place attention is drawn to their needs. They are at this point able to feel their emotions. The disadvantage is unlike others. Like the Fours, they may get stuck in depression which is maintained by seeing only what is missing in a particular relationship be it at work or within their social circles. Their skills though are to center inside oneself and to know what they want or to develop a sort of emotional intelligence, empowering the capacity of Twos for teamwork and networking. Being with point Four can assist them to find a home within themselves. In another direction, the point Eight would be the point of resource for these Twos. Irrespective of whether it is productive they may depend on how the Twos are able to manage the assertive energy that is at Point eight. The question is whether they reach this point in a calm manner or whether they go off the rails. There are Twos that naturally just combine the going forward energy which is in their type with the assertion and taking charge energy that is found in the Eight. There are others who have a hard time going to Eight unless there is stress from the outside. Some access to point eight is good for learning to handle conflict, which usually does not come very easy.

Point three: wing designations

When the Two wing is predominant, then the Threes can be hospitable. They may bring their focus to networking in order to further their work. Successful connections made with other individuals are just a part of their program towards productivity. The Threes can display more people skills as compared to what be associated with those who are point Twos. They can sustain contact for a long time beyond a lot of personality modes in the enneagram. The problem is the way that both points reinforce dependency for the external approvals, trying to get recognized, which may create vanity.

Dynamic points

The relaxation stage for the point Threes is Six. This is where they feel like they can open space for introspection. For all of them, especially when they are in places of leadership, the skill is to pose queries and understand opposing forces. This comes from point Six and is needed for success in the long term along with effectiveness. Point Six takes on objectives and encourages informed decision making.

Point four wing points

When the Three wing is predominant, the Fours will then consider the external environment. They have the ability to work with Threes in order to achieve a good amount of success in their business operations. They are able to place aside a lot of individualism to blend in, while still keeping personalized touches within their presentation. They can meet the expectations of others but they will usually feel tension concerning their social life and public representation. When the Five wing is predominant then the four will seek tasks which have time for them to introspect.

Dynamic points

The point of relaxation for the Fours would be point One. When they are feeling appreciated then the gravity would shift to the body center. They get very calm emotionally at this point. They do not have a lot of mood swings. The feelings of sadness and longing transforms into the One point which is backed by a sense of practical activity. The point Fours would like to pace things that are right, rather than consider what is wrong. The resource point for the Fours would be point Two. The Fours usually say that it is stressful to stay in this forward moving point for a long time. It can begin to feel pretentious as if they feel like they are giving up individuality to win approval and make personal connection. The Fours are able to accept they are going out of their comfort zone to an external setting that would work better as opposed to feeling forced to socialize.

Point five wing point

When the point Four wing is predominant then the Fives have an active emotional lifestyle. Even though the emotions can be hard to see, they are still quite valid and this places a direct influence on behavior. The challenge would be integration of feeling functions, so they are not pulling in different directions or creating tension. While the Four wing can support interpersonal warmth, it may also lead to disjointed styles. When the Sixth wing is the predominant one, the activity of the mental center is the one which is reinforced. There happens to be strong focus on technical data here with systems of information as the solution to life issues. The problem is that the Fives are prone to worry which threatens problems to be larger than they actually are.

Dynamic points

Point Eight is the relaxation point. Quiet and withdrawn, the individual may become body centered and even excessive in the way they express themselves. Both the Eight and the Five points are self-referencing and so it is not easy for one to hear or include the feelings of another person. Though, it comes with a lot of good energy if managed in the right manner. The resource point for the Five is point seven. On the other hand, point Seven allows the Five to be more outgoing. They can become the life of the party when their enthusiasm is engaged.

Point six wing points

When the Five wing is the predominant one, then the Sixes are going to want to keep their privacy as the main priority. They might be a bit reserved in social situations unless they know the people who are there. They also have a tendency to want to know everything about a scenario before taking action. The Seven wing on point Six ,propels the Sixes toward participation in experiences which are enjoyable. In the same manner as the Sevens, they can create plans and options provided where they are unaware of what the limits are.

Dynamic points

The relaxation point for the Sixes is point Nine. That would be illustrated when they drop their gravity center to the belly. They have a habit of scanning their surroundings in order to anticipate problems, finding out what risks are present. The point Three is the resource point for the Sixes. This allows the Sixes the chance of achieving actions more immediately than usual for their personality type. As opposed to being guided by rules, the Three energy is responsive and adaptable.

Point seven wing point

When the Six wing is the predominant one the Sevens get reinforced. They may become engrossed in everything that is going on that they rarely pay attention to their wellbeing. They also have the capacity to plan and visiualise with a lot of mental speed. When the Eighth wing is the predominant one, then the Sevens get pulled to more physical experiences. They may become very good adventurers even if it concerns business ventures, partying or sports. The expansive nature of both points can make them a bit restless and have them doing things that make them feel relevant.

Dynamic points

The relaxation point for point Seven would be point Five. The interesting thing is that when the sevens feel they are safe and secure they are able to remediate to their attention style of up and out. They may retreat within themselves and become very reflective. However a lot of Sevens understand there is big benefit in being able to center inside of oneself in order to quiet the mind and to think in a clear manner, withdrawing from the flow of activity. The resource point for point Sevens is point One. Because the Sevens are usually situated in a position of being okay when others are okay, their point allows them to be critical, causing their actions to have to be done in the right manner. When they are placed in this position by the stress they experience, they may exhibit attributes of point One, like being judgmental and resentful.

Point eight wing points
When Seven is the predominant one, the Eight can be a charming individual and very outgoing. They tend to embrace adventure and risk at this situation. They also have a lot of access to vitality and even aggression. This energy can enable them to be very good at business or contracting. In contrast, the Nine wing allows the eights to be laid back. They can exercise strength and control at this stage. Their energy is usually much quieter as compared to the other Eights that may give the impression that they are not aggressive in the first case.

Dynamic points
The Two is the relaxation point for the Eight. At this juncture, they are able to adequately access their emotions; which is not very easy for the Eight. To a certain point the Eight has concentrated their assertion and defenses to consider a world filled with a lot of conflict, it entails courage to open up to be seen as being vulnerable. The emotions of people can be hidden in the right way, releasing energy and allowing for a lot of motivation for better or worse.
The resource point for point Eight is point Five. This is a go-to point for the Eights that look for privacy on a daily basis. They also need their own space and instead of their mode of going into activity, the Five just allows them to strategize and go into quiet reflection. The Eight may over invest in a lot of things, meaning a

bit of detachment may be quite helpful to them. Though if they stay too long at this point, they can then become shut down and melancholic.

Point Nine wing points

When Eight is the predominant wing, the Nine can adopt attributes which are very methodical and exact from others around them. The Nines with a One wing are going to feel motivated to go along with the expectations of the Ones that are in authority. They will just not keep up with the compliance in the same thorough manner as the ones and they may forget or act out in a passive aggressive manner. The other predominant wing for the Nine is the Eight which brings the Nine into their rebellious side. With this wing, the Nine can be more assertive as compared to their cousins with the One wing.

Dynamic points

The Three is the point of relaxation. At this time, the Nine can be in a more active feeling area. This can be overwhelming which allows the Nines to derive questions about who they are and what their true identities are. The resource point though for the Nine would be the Six. When the Nine becomes motivated by events that are outside their control, they go to this point. Their perception becomes much sharper and instead they are able to zero in on what the problem is at the time.

Chapter Two: Personality Types

People vary physically, meaning you can distinguish one person from the other through various features such as their skin complexions, their hair, their height, their weight, and their shapes amongst others. That said, we could classify them further and group those who share these traits together and give them names as we did blonds, blacks, white, and tall.

The same way we classify people with their physical attributes we can classify them with their individual and particular personalities. There is a reason why the world is as it is, why we attain certain achievements in life, why we excel in different areas in life, why we handle situations as we do, why some relationships last and some don't, why we handle pain differently and why some people are more social than others. Our personalities, determine a lot in a person because the shape our attitudes towards different stimuli in our environments. This eventually alters our approach and reactions to such circumstances.

Personalities are the people we are or rather the kind of personality we possess and this affects the way we relate to each other. For example you meet a person covered in tattoos and dreadlocks. One person may assume they are immoral individuals with no respect for religion and therefore dangerous. Another person may think that its rather impressive, attractive and that he or she has an artistic and creative personality. These different reactions are drawn because of the different personalities within us. This can also apply in our relationships, normally unlike people attract and end up having amazing relationships and this is where people will say "opposites attract". However, imagine a case where no one was different or special?.. What you stand for is what the next person stands for and the other and the other. Naturally this would bore you to death, listening to the same songs, loving the same things, doing the same careers, having the same opinions and so on. At first this all sounds so interesting and fun but if you contextualize it and put it into perspective, you realize that with time it becomes overwhelming and boring. Then there would be no point of conversing because no different ideologies are being exchanged just the same old things redundantly. This would kill so many relationships as there is no excitement or exploration of different perspectives between people and life. This challenging no purpose and no fulfillment, just reciprocity everywhere, meaning itself would be lost in life.

Another area that will be affected by this is our careers because we are moved by the same stimuli pushing us into wanting to achieve the same goals which isn't necessarily a bad thing but can lead to stagnation as there are so many areas in life that need to be tapped into and exploited. We all have a purpose in life and that's what makes some of us politicians, chefs, bankers and others entrepreneurs.

We are pushed by different things and moved by different stimuli leading us to our destined paths, where we are also pushed differently to achieve or reach different levels of our chosen paths. That is the reason why some end up in management, some stagnate, some starts rival businesses and some opt out and choose different paths in life. Our personalities shape our thinking, attitudes, perceptions, beliefs and behaviors. They make us who we are. They make life what it is.

There are various groupings of personalities and they are grouped together because of their strongest traits or the one thing about them that stands out most. We'll look at each of the Nine groupings and how it affects the people towards relations, success, purpose and overall approach what they face in life.

Type 1: The Perfectionist

The perfectionist, just as their name suggests, they are always keeping it 100. In whatever aspect of life, they do it to the best of their ability, they take life very seriously and whatever tasks the take on they either do it perfectly or don't do it at all. With type Ones, there in no in-between.. They are honest, dependable and use common sense. What this basically means is that they will make great efforts in straightening the conditions around them.

Whatever seems off they would go extra miles to put it back to how it should be even if it is a small change to something.

The challenge comes when their point of view isn't attainable or when what they are trying to change cannot be changed. This drives a hole through them because they are idealistic and believe that everything should be complete and in perfect accuracy. This is a big challenge that affects their perceptions and attitudes towards different aspects of their lives.

For example, in relationships they might try to make their partners see things as they do and try making them have a common point of view with them towards everything. This, in most cases, would make them vulnerable to being prideful and might come off as rude or arrogant possibly leading them to poor relationships and interactions. The ability to take and receive information willingly from different parties is what makes communication and relations what they are and adds meat to the bone. Having a strong minded individual who has strong beliefs about what he knows can be very frustrating at times and can drive away interest or lead to arguments that are pointless, especially if they are wrong.

Their purpose in life in general can also have its fair share of effects from their personality. By this I mean that because they do not accept less than perfect and struggle taking others' opinions they might end up wasting their time, money and energy into trying to prove facts that are nonexistent. Causing them to chase dead causes and since they don't share freely, end up suffering emotionally and psychologically, keeping all of their hurt within themselves and refusing to share.

It isn't all bad though because their perfectionist nature serves them well at most times as they tend to be honest and responsible, meaning they often try and get their facts right and raise the standards of those around them. They take full responsibility of their actions, making them reliable people to turn to for advice because they tend to see reality for what it is; right from wrong, good from bad and black from white. Their clarity is essential in life and offers a clear perspective of their journey, allowing them to assess what works and what doesn't work. This is a very important tool in life because life is all about improving and working on your flaws while dropping what doesn't work to attain the end product of being we intend or wish to be.

Type 2: The Giver

The second personality is the Giver, I can call them the "fit in" crew, since they like to seek human approval from amongst those they interact with. To them, approval is of utmost importance even if means making personal sacrifices on different things in their life. This personality is cautious of everything they say and can be good individuals to nurture and guide as they try seeing things from your perspective, accommodating or welcoming your thoughts, therefore giving you great advice and opinions on life. This though comes at a cost because having nothing you stand for can make you lose your identity as a person even if it benefits the other parties. The givers are very caring and they like to make sure everyone is 'okay' especially their friends and family. And also this is a very good trait, they can sometimes get stuck in situations where they believe everyone is selfish, however they made need to realize that they themselves need to be a little more selfish.

This affects different aspects of their lives, for example work, friendships and their relationships. They are very loving and accommodating people and the fact that they actually take time to know you and understand things as you see them, means that they are very good people to relate to. work with and have as friends. As said before this can have a down side where they may depend on people's approval. Lack of approval can then lead them to going into breakdowns and losing self-esteem, lowering their confidence in what they offer or bring to the table.

Independence of thought and having something you stand for brings about purpose and drive in an individual. Lack of that independence would mean someone is easily swayable and gullible, limiting his or her attitude and perception towards people in life. Some would argue that the Givers accommodative and adaptive nature makes them likeable and therefore more opportunities would be presented to them, this making them able to climb the corporate ladder faster than others would. They have a strong ability to welcome other people's ideas and thoughts causing people to view them as the go-to guy or girl. Givers solve anything that is put in front of them. And because of their socializing skills they are able to build a network faster than anyone else causing them to be greater at a lot of tasks, especially team based ones.

The giver may be dependent on other people as a source of happiness and success and this might lead him into being exploited for approval and taken advantage of. They can find themselves being naïve, thinking they are winning the trust and approval of others but they may be taken advantage of for the gain of others. This has a lot of hypocrisy in it and because of the constant change of personality to suit the situation, the giver might always struggle being appreciated for whom they truly are. Givers love to "give" and overall have an approachable and calming manner that others love to have around. They just need to be careful when being too nice, because some people out their take it for granted!

Type 3: The Performer

The third personality type is the Performer. He is goal oriented and hugely motivated allowing him or her to achieve great success. Their sole agenda is to make it in life because they are driven by being the odd one out. Most of the time they puts their success before their feelings, opinions and life. To them the best image they can portray of themselves is the revenge they can dish out for being sidelined. They are so obsessed with their image, they don't have time for other things in life which limits their scope and range, lacking to reach people.

They are high achievers mainly because they have dedicated most of their time and life into perfecting their craft. Because they are so focused on achieving their goals, following their dreams and passion, they can lead towards to developing health and psychological issue like fatigue, depression from possible lack of accomplishment. This may be because minimal time is spent taking care of their health and well-being and more on what they need to achieve career wise. The performer and the perfectionist share certain traits, for example, their obsession with achieving goals and doing it in the right way. This meaning that for the performer, nothing less than a hundred percent is accepted and this often leads them being very successful in whatever they do. They can also motivate themselves to overcome hurdles and push others to achieve their dreams and aspirations because they know what it entails. They're very good leaders and this make them exceptional at careers such as sports, acting and taking any entrepreneurial pathway.

The performer should allow life to take place, flow with it and experience all it has to offer. Accept all of its ups and down, and enjoy all experiences that they dive into, so they can draw their own conclusions in anything they tackle in life.

Type 4: The Romantic
The romantic type is about creativity and using art as a medium to channel their views, opinions and feelings. Different people have different ways in which we channel what is inside us. For some other personalities like the perfectionist they prefer keeping it within them and focusing on other things to stop thinking about their situations. The performer channels it to his work and through the high levels of success he attains.
On the other side the romantic has their own way of channeling his feelings, thoughts and attitudes. They do it through art, music, dance and poetry. Sentimental and elaborate when it comes to expressing their thoughts. They are passionate when moving between expressing what other people feel and what they themself feel. The romanticsare emotional individuals who comprehend emotion better than ant other personality group,

allowing them to reach other individuals who couldn't reach the comprehension point or understand their emotions through art.

Because of their emotional nature they need time to understand and accept whatever it is they are facing before they can welcome the world into their thoughts. They are very fragile and should be handled with care, because they carry so much emotion.

The romantic can be dynamic when it comes to mood in that he or she may be excited at times or dull depending on what he or she has on their plate at the time. They go through life with an open heart, ready for new experiences and they can take that with them on any task or career they want to tackle.

It's best for Romantics to balance between all emotions that occur and understand that they all happen for a reason. Doing this will draw different reactions for them, teaching them different things that help them develop better interactions and problem-solving skills.

Type 5: The Observer

The fifth personality we are going to look at is the Observer. These people are the introverts in society. They are keen on what takes place around them and do not accept things for what they are. They like to question everything they know and analyze their surroundings to draw meanings and conclusions to everything. The observer tends to dwell alone as he goes about formulating his ideologies. To him, family might be important, but his own interests are of more importance. They don't often indulge in small talk due to their introverted sociological environment and this is because they do not like sharing personal information and tend to keep a lot to themselves. They like to come up with conclusions and solutions from what they have experienced and from the various analyses they have found in their lives.

The observer does not like indulging in small talk and is more comfortable talking or discussing things that they actually excel at or expert in. This is because they fear what they don't know due to the fact that it makes them feel inferior and unknowledgeable. That said though they don't like sharing all the information the have about a particular topic of interest because they're advanced in it. Making it possible that they may be giving too much 'valuable' information away.

The Observers should drop down the walls they have built and share more, accepting more people in their life. This will help them avoid loneliness and also widen their range of knowledge, towards more things that they may be interested in life. Observers are very smart and are considered highly valuable people.

Type 6: The Loyal Skeptic

Two main things characterize this group: their ability to judge characters and situations and their ability to find solutions to problems before they occur. This category of people will always be on the lookout for people and situations that bring them harm and hurt to their families or loved ones. The simple reason being to them that people have different attitudes and intentions and it's up to them to figure them out and come up with quick solutions to whatever they might be. They do not trust easily but when they do, they trust very strongly, making them a great close friend because they will most definitely have your back.

The loyal skeptics are quick to come up with solutions and always remain ahead of the competition or situation, allowing them to be in control of their life making it easier for them to make decisions. They are strategic in how they come up with solutions because they either stop a problem or offer remedies to one empirically. They are courageous and selfless acting to ensure the safety and security of those they care about.

They are very attentive to people and situations because they are strategic. Every detail is relevant in coming up with control or preventive measures to whatever they face. They set high walls that others should prove beyond to protect their own emotional wellbeing from wrong people. They are brave, therefore ask serious questions, leading them to aggressive or pushy attitudes.

The Loyal- Skeptic should welcome more opinions and emotions to their lives and become more accommodating to everyone. This will allow them to grow as individuals, developing a sense of purpose holistically other than their careers just solely. Overall Type 6 is obviously very loyal making them a great friend and person to work with. They are very smart and love to protect those in their life who deserve to be protected.

Type 7: The Epicure
The seventh personality is the epicure, the dynamic crew. These are the ones that value freedom. They are in it for the experience, and they are driven by exploration. Type 7's want to visit different places, learn new things, explore different continents and live in the moment. They are never really stagnant.
This group of personalities are therefore always on the go achieving, realizing and exploring. It gives them so much exposure and make them good people to befriend and talk to because they have a scope of what to talk about and knowledge on the diversified cultures. This is why they should all be appreciated. They are generally very likeable people.
This group though is very uncommitted and undecided on what they want, they hop from one thing to another, and this gives them a sense of purpose and accomplishment, allowing them to draw meaning from their lives. They are all about what works for them and people's opinions don't really faze them. They tend to focus mostly on what they love and go about it whenever and however they see fit. They tend to have an attitude of avoiding their challenges and focus mainly on what's going on correctly. The Epicure group should try to accept that other people hold different opinions and feelings and they do to. Accepting this as a fact and understanding it entirely will help them develop better qualities and become better people all round.
Type 7's like to think as if 'Everything happens for a reason' and this is a powerful mindset to have.

Type 8: The Protector

The protectors often come out and speak on behalf of the rest. They have strong standings and beliefs causing them to be very assertive. They do not back down from a challenge and can be very aggressive and this can be both a good thing and a bad. They air the opinions and thoughts everyone else holds but cannot communicate. They believe that not standing for your rights and defending your opinions leads to exploitation and they term it as weakness.

Protectors are enthusiastic in that they are always on the ready no matter the situation. They await new situations that will come up against what they stand for and defend it fiercely and make sure their opinions are heard and respected by all. Type 8's are powerful people, allowing them to accomplish any task ahead of them. They also put facts as they are, without fear of contradiction. These individuals, like all the other personalities, have their downfalls, one of them being they are excessive. By this, we mean at times they cross certain lines trying to stand or fight for their rights. It's okay fighting for your rights and enjoying your freedom of expression but all things are done with both sides of the coin flipped. Where one person's rights start is where others end. These people might tend to cross this bridge knowingly or unknowingly from time to time.

The Protector can be quite dominant because their ideals and opinions were not supported. An attitude or perception may have been developed towards themselves if this is the case. Group 8's should try to understand cooperation and mutual understanding, as a means to resolve more issues and make their life easier.

Type 9: The Mediators

The final personalities are the Mediators. Here we have the best of both world's, defenders and challengers dependent on the scenario. The mediators main aim is to bring peace between two torn parties. This means they are welcoming to all opinions and suggestions as they aim to find a balance between all that is presented before them.

They are characterized positively by balance. They find the perfect balance between the two stories and draw sensible or workable conclusions that are accepted by both parties. Secondly, they are accepting, by this I mean that they consider other people's points of view and try to see where they are coming from and why they think as they do. Lastly, they are harmonious, meaning that their main aim is to draw a reasonable and acceptable conclusion to issues and phenomenon in the calmest manner possible.

With positives also comes negative and type 9's have their down sides like all the rest despite their calm and approachable nature. Firstly, they are stubborn because of their drive to get information for resolution provision, they persist an issue until a situation is fully settled and they are also conflict avoidant. They aim to avoid conflict completely, even if at times it might be the best way to find a resolution and this can be cause due to their fear of the situation escalating and going out of hand.

Mediators offer solutions and are open to ideas and opinions which make them standout in a group. The mediators should understand that at times conflict management is essential in drawing conclusions and getting solutions to most issues in society right now.

All these different personalities are what give life its essence. The personality of an individual as seen affects almost everything in life from the way we understand things, relate to people the way we solve situations. Ignorance can make one think that someone is rude or someone else is easy going. Understanding that people handle things differently and taking time to appreciate it and understand it puts a lot of perspective into human life and allows us to tap into human potential. It's important to accept the environment, as it is where everyone is given equal chances to be whom he or she is and express themselves in whatever way. Each personality has its own strengths and weakness and understanding that will allow you to drive further action in life and build greater relationships.

Chapter Three: Personality Type Test

The Riso Hudson Enneagram type indicator will assist you with finding your enneagram type if you're not exactly sure which type resonated with you earlier. This test was initiated by Don Richard Riso and Russ Hudson in 1993 and the research particularly focused on the construction of Rheti, which was the main personality measuring instrument.

Over the course of time, it has been found to be of heuristic value but there is minimal research on a scientific basis, which has been done on the matter. Some of the first steps in the validation of the Riso Hudson enneagram type indicator were made by Warling after collecting information from 153 students that completed the RHETI. More information on the RHETI was done by Dameyer, who showed that retesting and reliability was at a high rate when 82 percent of the people he tested were seen to have the same type they had when they completed the questionnaire a second time.

While a number of enneagram questionnaires have been developed and may show a reasonable amount of reliability, the validity is a bit harder to believe. Utilizing the personality questionnaire as a measure for the enneagram type of an individual can be quite tricky. Part of what makes it so useful when it comes to application is the part where it describes the conscious processes and the motivations that one would not have a lot of access to.

While it is still possible to use the questionnaires the most reliable way is to use the self-assessment questionnaires.

Reliable criterion measures

You should note there are no right answers and no personality type is better than the other. Attempt to answer the questions to the best of your ability in the most honest way possible also. You ought not analyze the questions or think of the exceptions to the rule. You have to be spontaneous and choose the statement which comes closest to the way you have been a lot of your life. If there is difficulty in discovering the personality type because two or more scores are close, then you may find it helpful for you to discuss responses with those who know you very well like a friend, a parent or even a spouse.

There are 38 queries within the sample test. In each case, you need to select the answer which best applies to your scenario. You may skip questions which do not apply though you should not skip questions because they are hard. This test usually takes a duration of about 5 to 10 minutes. For each of the questions they are divided into two options. You need to answer with a designation as A, B, C, D, E, F, G, H, I.

Important:

The table below is the illustration of how the enneagram test works. You are supposed to select one option per question from A to I according to the intensity of agreement. In this way it functions like a Likert scale where A would take the position of the least agreement and I would represent the option for agreeing the most. So in the first question, if you claim to be extremely imaginative and funny then the option taken would be I. Though since my option for this is less agreement, I would go for B. Every question has been answered and marked with a 1 according to the individual's preference for the question. The results are then tabulated as the sum of the answers at the bottom of the graph. In the graph below, the results at the bottom of the chart shows the enneagram type of the individual and they have been illustrated as an example.

From this illustration we can see the top figures are 11, 17 and 13 from options C, D and E.

where we garner the logic of the use of the chart rows of A to I. Each letter from A, B, C, D, E, F, G, H and I represents a personality type as shown in the table below

Columns	A	B	C	D	E	F	G	H	I
Numerical Values									
Personality Type	Nine	Six	Three	One	Four	Two	Eight	Five	Seven

That means that in the example given since D is the most prominent in the results, the enneagram type One is the most prominent for this person doing the test.
So you have a clearer idea, here is an illustration of the test that this person filled in so you have a better idea of how it works:
And don't forget that at the end of this book, there is a clear table where you can work out your own personality type!

		Type	9	6	3	1	4	2	8	5	7	
		Disagree	A	B	C	D	E	F	G	H	I	Agree
1	I have been imaginative and romantic.					1						
	I have been down to earth and pragmatic.						1					
2	I have a tendency to avoid confrontation.							1				
	I have a tendency to go into confrontations.									1		
3	I have usually been direct, idealistic and formal.					1						
	I have usually been diplomatic, ambitious and charming.					1						
4	I have tried to be intense and focused.				1							
	I have a tendency to be fun loving and spontaneous.						1					
5	I am a private person and have not tried to mi1 a lot with other people.								1			
	I have been hospitable as an individual and enjoyed welcoming friends to my life.								1			
6	Generally, it has been hard to get a rise so to speak from me.										1	

#	Statement	1	2	3	4	5	6	7	8	9	10
	Generally, it has been easy to get a rise from me.									1	
7	I have been a high-minded idealist.								1		
	I have been more of a street-smart person or idealist.							1			
8	I have needed to give people affection.							1			
	I have had the preference of maintaining particular distance with individuals.									1	
9	I have needed to give people affection.							1			
	I have had the preference of maintaining particular distance with individuals.							1			
10	When given a chance at a new e1perience, I have asked myself whether I would enjoy it.						1				
	When presented with new e1periences I have asked mostly whether it would be useful to me.							1			
11	I have had the tendency of focusing too much on my needs.							1			
	I am one of those people that focuses mostly on other people.					1					
12	I come across as being too unsure of things and myself.								1		
	I give off the vibe that I am too sure of myself								1		

13	Other people have depended on the decisiveness and the strength that I give out.									1				
	Other people have depended on the knowledge and insight that I give out.											1		
14	I tend to be more goal oriented as opposed to being relationship oriented.												1	
	I tend to be more relationship oriented than goal oriented.													1
15	I am not very able to speak up for myself.												1	
	I am very outspoken and so I have said what others have wished that they had the nerve to say.											1		
16	It is difficult for me to become more fle1ible and to take things easier.									1				
	It has been hard for me to stop alternatives and to do something which is definite.								1					
17	I have a tendency for procrastination and to be hesitant.					1								
	I have a tendency for being domineering and being courageous.							1						
18	My eagerness to have others depend on me has severally gotten me in trouble with them.									1				
	My hesitation to get involved a lot has gotten me into trouble with other people.								1					
1	Usually, I have had the ability to put										1			

#	Statement	1	2	3	4	5	6	7	8	9	10	11
9	feelings aside and to get the task at hand done.											
	Usually, I have had to work through my emotions before I could get things done.								1			
20	Usually, I am adventurous and have taken risks.								1			
	Usually I am quite meticulous and cautious.										1	
21	I have had tendencies to be serious as a reserved person that likes to discuss things.								1			
	I have tended to be supporting as a giving person that likes the company of other people.							1				
22	I have usually felt the need to perform in the right manner.								1			
	I have often gotten the need to be a pillar of stability.							1				
23	I have been interested usually in the maintenance of stability and peace.										1	
	I have been interested usually in asking tough queries while maintaining some independence.								1			
24	I am very soft hearted and sentimental.				1							
	I am skeptical and hard-nosed in thought processes.				1							
25	I have worried a lot that if I let my guard down that other people are going to take advantage.						1					
	I have worried that I am missing out on connections							1				

#	Statement	1	2	3	4	5	6	7	8	9	10	11	12	13	14
	with other people.							1							
26	My habit of telling others what to do is annoying to my loved ones.							1							
	My habit of being isolated has put others off.								1						
27	Usually when troubles have gotten the best of me, I have treated myself to relieve the stress.										1				
	Usually when troubles have gotten to me, I have been able to work and eventually tune them out.								1						
28	I have not depended on individuals as I have done things solely by myself.							1							
	I have depended on friends and they have known they have the ability to depend on me.								1						
29	I have had the tendency to be self-absorbed and moody.												1		
	I have tendencies to be detached and preoccupied.									1					
30	I like to comfort others when they are distressed and calm them down.								1						
	I like to challenge other people and to shake them up.									1					
31	I have been a serious and earnest or self-disciplined individual.							1							
	I have been a serious a carefree and sociable individual.						1								

#	Statement						A	B	C	D	E	F	G	H	I
32	I have liked to let people know about my strengths or what I can do well.									1					
	I have been very shy about telling others about my strengths and abilities.							1							
33	Having comfort and security is more important to me as compared to pursuing personal interests and preferences.						1								
	Pursuing personal interests has been more significant than having comfort or security.							1							
34	When I have had conflict with other people, I back down on rare occasions.									1					
	When I have had conflict with other individuals, I tended to back down or withdraw.									1					
35	I have been known for my sense of humor and unsinkable optimistic attitude.								1						
	I have been known for my quiet strength and e1ceptional amount of generosity as an individual.							1							
36	A lot of success has been because of talent in making a good impression								1						
	A lot of success has been attained despite the lack of interest in development of interpersonal skills.							1							
						Total	2	9	1	11	17	1	9	6	3	2
						Column	A	B	C	D	E	F	G	H	I
						Type	9	6	3	1	4	2	8	5	7

In this case, this person is most strongest in Column D so their Personality type would be Type 1: The Reformer.

Columns	A	B	C	D	E	F	G	H	I
Numerical Values									
Personality Type	Nine	Six	Three	One	Four	Two	Eight	Five	Seven

The following chart shows an example enneagram results for the same test done by another person.

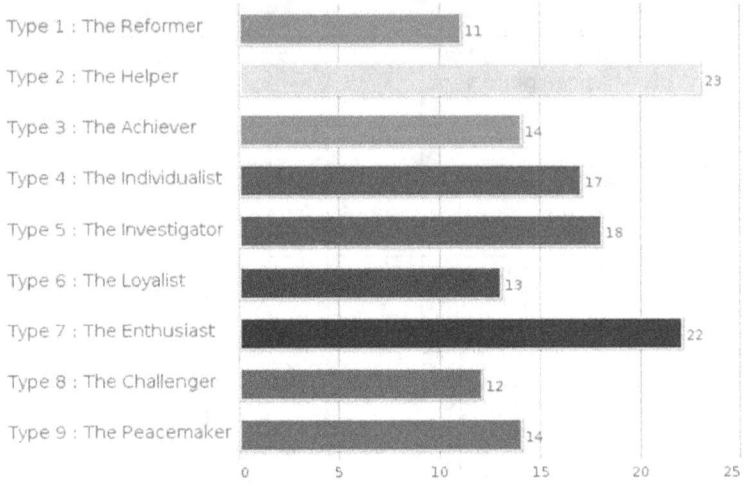

The discovery of which of the nine types represents one's personality type would be the objective of this test. In the event that you have provided an honest answer for each query which tests a different aspect of your personality, then the accurate type should be displayed as one of the top three scores. If done the right way, the Riso Hudson Enneagram type indicator is going to accurately assess your basic personality type. If the results are not clear, then you need to review your responses as well from an arithmetic point of view. Remember that the questionnaire has 36 questions which are divided into two segments so the total of the answers should be 72.

Remember at the end of this book, there is a clear table where you can work out your personality type!

Chapter Four: Subtypes (27)

Once you have figured out your specific Personality type or maybe you already know what it is. It is now time to have a look at the Subtypes within each Type. These are extra traits within each personality type; you can explore these and take advantage of them for yourself and to better understand the others around you.
There are basic instinctual drives which are necessary for all human experience and they reside in everyone as a primal force. They can be distinguished from personality and often operate from the subconscious yet they are very strong in the direction of how we are as individuals. Though these instincts there are usually, one of the three that may become more dominant. When the main instinct arises with the core enneagram type then a new attribute character is formed.
Take for example if the enneagram was a plate of food then the instinct would determine what you eat first or last. That then relates to the belief of what is good for us or what is thought to be needed in order to get what we want and require in the world. These instincts concern the fundamental intelligences which have come up to make sure people have survived the continuation of the human species. Recent advances in the field of neuroscience have shown the unseen way that these instincts show themselves in the modern world. Now each type of the enneagram personality types has three associated instinctual subtypes that will be mentioned. These are: self-preservation, one on one and the social or sexual element.
The following text will go through how each type is assimilated into the subtypes with consideration for these three elements.

Type 1

Self-preservation : Controlling

The true embodiment of the perfectionist is someone that has a tendency to fuss a lot over everything and wants to make sure that everything is under control. The subtype key under the self-preservation element in the perfectionist is Worry, which should exacerbate the character itself. The worry element for the type Ones makes them have a strong inner critic which piles on to their self-doubt and strict retentiveness. They become excessively hard on themselves and have a heightened sense of responsibility. They may become very anxious and they do not like to entertain deviances even if it is the smallest detail. Unfortunately, it does not come with an aggressive outlet, which would be advisable as this subtype avoids the expression of anger. They can feel very frustrated when they experience any form of disruption in their activities.

One on one: Stand Out

The subtype key for the perfectionist is they stand out. The reason is their effect on other people. This subtype key allows for an idealistic perspective concerning the way that things need to be causing them to have a sense of entitlement on the way things have to be. It may also make them feel entitled to make others fall into the way they would envision something or someone, putting pressure on others to go according to the way they would like. This subtype key may express anger especially when their efforts to fix the situation are ignored or face resistance.

Social: Non- Adaptable

The subtype key for the perfectionist is being non adaptable. The perfectionist is the one that brings attention to what is right, good and appropriate so they set an example for principled activities. However, this has a flip side as they also have a tendency to be uncompromising even when it comes to the smallest things. High self-discipline and standards are the things that set them apart from the ones that are around them. They are highly motivated by things such as fairness and making things to be in the right way. When they are at their best, they can be systematic thinkers and therefor make very good role models.

Type 2

Self-preservation: Privilege

The subtype key for the giver is referred to as Privilege for the self-preservation element. They are childlike in a way where they can be a bit shy but they can also be charming which makes others want to protect them. The privileged giver is one that wants others to take care of them but does not want to depend fully on others. This making them very protective of their emotions and protective in taking on long term commitments.

One on one: Seduction

The element of one on one inspires the subtype towards seduction, which focuses on the seductive abilities and energies that they attract in intimate relationships. When they are in close relationships with others, they can feel secure and be able to claim what they need in a clear and assertive manner. Though they are gentle, they can be very strong willed and passionate, finding themselves wild at heart. They are also very devoted within these close relationships and they may find it hard to accept boundaries or limits they can go to. As such, it can be a bit hard for them to take no for an answer.

Social: Ambition

The subtype key for the social element in the giver is ambition. The Giver utilizes their strengths in an intelligent way in order to attract and engage communities and broader systems. They may even stand out towards a central or leadership role. They enjoy being with the crowd or up to date with the latest information. The weakness of giving more than they get could be an adapted in a way to distract them from feeling awkward.

Type 3

Self-preservation: Security

The subtype key for the self-preservation element in the achiever is the countertype security. This is a countertype where they do not like advertising strengths and accomplishments in an open manner and they may avoid to be seen as wanting attention. In spite of this matter it is significant for them to be known for their hard work. They have a reliable and efficient subtype and they tend to work towards the right way to do things. They also pursue stability and self-security through their work which may lead to them being workaholics.

One on one: Charisma

The Charismatic subtype of the one on one element for the achiever may focus on their competitiveness towards seeing successful outcomes in other individuals. They usually believe that if the ones around them are to be successful then they should be too. They may also tend to look for affections and the attention of the ones that are closest to them while suppressing their own comfort so that they can host the expectations of others.

Social: Prestige

The social aspect of three has a subtype of prestige as they desire influence and tend to have skills in adjusting to the social requirements of groups and corporations. They are very competitive as they enjoy being the center of attention and confidently market themselves. They work towards being known for their performance and accomplishments. Looking the best and being successful is a very important aspect for the type three social.

Type 4

Self-preservation: Tenacity

The individualist self-preservative is one that is quite resourceful. They suffer stoically and want to be recognized for being able to stomach a lot and not complain. Even if they are very sensitive and might be detached from their feelings, they prefer not to share their issues with other people. This subtype for type 4's have a lot of empathy and they do their best to support people who they believe are experiencing suffering.

One on one: Competition

Individualist's are very intense and can raise their voice to champion their needs and feelings. The subtype of competition for the Type Four can be demanding causing them to escape negative fates by being the best at what they do. They demand that others appreciate the needs they have which can be counter-productive and lead to frustration and anger.

Social: Shame

The social four is very sensitive and connected to the roots of their suffering. There is comfort in the manner that they suffer and they usually attract the admiration from other people. They really want to be understood and this can manifest in self-doubt. This subtype for type 4's can make a comparison to another individual and end up blaming themselves for things that they can or cannot control.

Type 5

Self-Preservation: Castle

The reason why the subtype of the self-preservation type 5 is the castle is because they enjoy their personal space to an extra level. They set out a lot of boundaries and they can live solitary lives with only a few friends. They rather watch social life pass by than participate in it because they enjoy their own company. They are true introverts and prefer not showing a lot of their inner selves, finding it hard to lower their guard without losing a bit of their privacy.

One on one: Confidant

The subtype for the investigator is one that focuses on one or two people in a life that is mostly reserved. They have a strong chemistry with another person and enjoy the connections, however they may live variously through them in some cases. This can lead them to decide to test the loyalty of their partners or resist the potential of them having to be shared with other people.

Social: Totem

The type five social focuses on the big picture and usually looks for the essence and meaning of situations. They tend to connect with experts and groups that have similar high idealism and ones that are detached from the everyday problems or emotions. This subtype for type 5's share values with a lot of enthusiasm, however they still want a big part of their privacy kept to them selves. This may cause them to resist sharing space, or inner resource thus detaching from their environment.

Type 6

Self-preservation: Warmth

In order to feel security, this subtype for type 6's do their best to build alliances and strong relationships with other people. They are very warm in the manner they interact with other people but this is all pointed so that they get what they want in the end. They also repress anger or hesitate to give their honest stand on things as they have a preference to be cautious when at slight risk.

One on One: Intimidation

This subtype for type 6's can come as being quite intimidating and this could lead for one to misdiagnose them as a person. The Six one on one is believed to have a good defense and an even better offense. This approach means they can tackle a lot of situations, especially ones that they initiate and this why other may be a little shy around them.

Social: Duty

This subtype key for the type six is known as Duty. This connects to the usual ideals such as working for a particular cause or even standing up for those who are disadvantaged in society. This subtype key tends to see things in a more polarized manner as compared to the compromising Sixes. They are highly precise and careful and have a preference for following rules and procedure.

They also work to encourage compliance to the regulations or the collective norms, making sure that everyone knows the things that are expected of them.

Type 7

Self-Preservation: Network

The energized version of the type seven is someone that knows how to network. They have a family of supporters as they tend to be motivated by wanting what is best for everyone around them. They have a good sense of how to take care of themselves as they like the good things in life. This subtype for type 7's can be very good at rationalizing and defending themselves as well.

One on one: Fascination

The one on one Seven is one that looks at reality through the eyes of the idealist and connects this to every possibility. Their sense of optimism and enthusiasm could be naïve or unrealistic because they want to see the good in everything and everyone. This could make them a possible easy target for people who choose to take advantage of their goodness.

Social: Sacrifice

This is the countertype that works against self-interest for the type Seven. They are very generous and could be confused as a giver as they have strong ideals to be of service in order to create a world which is better. They are willing to sacrifice their needs in order to satisfy those of a larger group that they support. In the end, they can be a bit judgmental concerning selfishness when it comes to them or other individuals. The social subtype for type 7's, highly value being appreciated for the sacrifices that they make for the good of the group.

Type 8

Self-Preservation: Satisfaction

The type 8 self-preservation subtype is one that is productive and seems to be very effective. They seem to be confident even in situations, which are challenging. They play the role of the guardian angel for a lot of people as they seem like a pillar of fortitude. However when their needs are not being met they can become resentful and intolerant. Making a no-nonsense approach so that they get what they want without having to apologize or feel any guilt.

One on one: Possession

This subtype represents the most rebellious archetype of the type Eight which is quite provocative, breaking the rules as they please. They are very impulsive and have a desire to be intense making them willing to disrupt and provoke others if to accumulate influence and power. They also have the desire to serve a cause, which is worthy as long as it's from a point where they are leaders.

Social: Solidarity

The social type Eight is one that utilizes their influence in serving other people and drive for the support of other people. They can be very sensitive to injustice and social norms, which are not fair to everyone as they are loyal and protective, especially towards their close friends. Even though they have a preference of not being very vulnerable they also invite good feedback from people that are close to them.

Type 9

Self-preservation: Appetite

This subtype for personality type 9 self-preservation is known as appetite. This is concerned with the needs of the body center with such activities like eating or sleeping for their wellbeing and comfort. They like to use activities, which are a strategy towards comfort for themselves through the fulfillment of their appetites. Peace and time alone are some of the significant things that they need because they value their privacy. They can be irritable especially when other people come into their area and upset the balance of things.

One on one: Fusion

The subtype key for the one on one Nine fuses strongly with others in relationships so that they can feed their sense of comfort and themselves. They are much more secure when they are in romantic relationships or when they are partnered with others because they find it hard to do things by themselves. They are not likely to pay attention to their desires and passions as they get caught up in going along with the preferences of other people, even if it would mean the sacrifice of their needs.

Social: Participation

The social subtype key for the nine participates and regularly becomes the mediator or the one that facilitates in groups. They place their issues aside and maintain a happy look in order to avoid having to burden other people. They make sacrifices in order to meet the needs of the group because they gain a lot of comfort from being part of things in bigger groups. They work hard to keep those in their life happy, however they may encounter potential risk of becoming a workaholic, hiding their pain in their stresses.

Chapter Five: Self-Awareness And Growth Through Your Personality Type

Now that you have discovered your personality type, it is important that you consider actions and steps that will allow you the joys of personal growth to become more self-aware. As you would guess, different personalities have different actions and recommendations for the journey of self-awareness. Therefore, let us examine each of these individually in order to help you identify what works best for your type.

1. Type One: The Reformer

The main concern for you is to reclaim your serenity and learn to be Zen. In order for you to grow as a person, you must learn to release your resistance and accept that just because things do not seem to be perfect it does not mean that they are bad or unworthy. In order to achieve this, it is advisable that you relax; taking time for yourself and release the mental burden that you need to do everything. It might be difficult to start but you need to understand that what you do not accomplish or do, will not always result in a disaster of chaos. Even though it feels like you are the savior of the world, it is not the case and therefore you should not push to be Superman.

As a type One, you should learn to embrace not only your imperfections but those of others as well. This will help you when resolving conflicts with others as you will become more open minded to the opinions of others. Doing this will allow you to be more forgiving of mistakes, which can help you as a giver of knowledge. Speaking of knowledge, because you have a natural talent of teaching others, it is important to learn to be patient especially when it comes to change. You may embrace change quickly but for the ones you teach, it might not come as easy. However, it does not mean that it will never happen.

Use positive affirmations to guide you such as 'Life is perfect as it is', 'I choose to be flexible, adaptable and embrace change', and 'I choose to be kind, compassionate and understanding'. This will help you get in touch with your emotions while still maintaining the intelligent, reasonable, and logical side that is in you.

2. Type Two: The Helper

If you are a helper seeking personal growth, your area of concern should be to reclaim humility through becoming more conscious of your own motives. To start, you should learn to differentiate between meeting your needs and not being too needy; it will stop you from being clingy and turn you into an emotionally aware person.

Because you give love unconditionally, you do well in relationships. However, it may often draw you away from taking care of your own needs because you are too concerned with fulfilling your partner's needs. Keep your genuine loving nature but also put in more effort into caring for yourself and meeting your needs first.

As it has already been established, you enjoy helping others and it is a spirited nature that you should continue to do. You can adjust it slightly in two main ways; first, ask people what they really need before doing something for them or helping them. Second, fight the temptation of reminding people what you have done for them after you have done it. Instead, let it be and leave it to them to either thank you or not, rather than reminding them and making them feel uneasy. Your positive affirmations should range between loving others and yourself unconditionally and being perfectly clear about your intentions.

3. Type Three: The Achiever

An achiever's true growth and self-development comes in the form of being truthful. This starts with being honest with yourself and others, especially about your feelings. Be authentic by resisting the temptation to brag or impress others. Take some time off from your busy day to connect with another person you care about; it will allow you to become more loving and caring in your relationships.

Your ambition is a great quality that you should hold on to; you can improve this by allowing yourself regular breaks to not exhaust yourself. These breaks give you the opportunity to get in touch with yourself and recharge your batteries. Taking a break will also help you understand that success does not rest on your shoulders alone; allowing you to consider making a team.

Develop yourself through avoiding doing what is acceptable just to be accepted; take time to discover your values instead. The most important positive affirmation you should repeat to yourself is that you are authentic despite your mistakes and imperfections.

4. Type Four: The Individualist

The most important thing for you is to understand that your feelings are not a true source of support. That being said, try avoid working according to your mood; meaningful work should not wait until you are in the right mood. No matter how small the contribution may be, making contributions through work will help you discover your talents and special skills.

In order to develop your self-confidence, you should bury the feeling of 'not being together' and put yourself in the path of good. The best way to do this is to take on a challenge whether it be physically or emotionally; at work or in a relationship- the commitment will bring out the best in you. If the challenge gets you stressed, you should give yourself time and space to de-stress through communicating with your loved ones.

As much as you may enjoy lengthy conversations in your imagination, you should take it down a notch and instead use this time to build relationships with your loved ones through actual conversations. Practice equanimity and find joy in the present.

5. Type Five: The Investigator

For type five, you receive spiritual growth and self-awareness when you give yourself to others. It is normal to have conflicts and you should allow yourself to work things out; it will make you work well when it comes to resolving conflicts. Having even one friend whom you are comfortable conflicting with is a real bonus to your personal growth.

Because you are so intense, it may be difficult to unwind and let go; this can easily lead to unhealthy ways of coping with stress such as drug abuse and alcohol. When you get stressed, turn to exercise or biofeedback techniques; it will turn your nervous energy into helpful motivation to keep at it.

Your mental capacity is indeed an extraordinary gift but it can take you out of the here and now. Possibly drowning you in your mental capacity. Try as much as possible to stay with your physicality by speaking out your thoughts and ideas with others around you. This will not only make you a better communicator but it will also help you get your needs met.

6. Type Six: The Loyalist

Your spiritual path as a type six is to let go of fear because after all, you attract what you think. Learn to be present in your own anxiety because after all, people are more anxious than you think and it is not unusual. If you get in touch with your anxiety and pick up on it, you will be able to manage it and may even be able to turn it into a powerful tonic that energizes you and makes you more productive.

When under stress, you may find yourself to be testy, angry, or simply competitive. This can make you blame others for your own shortcomings; therefore, become aware of your pessimism and find creative ways of dealing with it. Learn to point out what makes you overreact and learn to manage your thoughts about these topics. You should always remind yourself that things are not as bad as they seem and that the 'bad' is mostly your imagination overreacting. Managing this helps you solve problems faster and in a more logical way.

Trust is a big issue for this type of personality but in order for you to grow; you need to become more trusting. Look for people in your life who care about you and have themselves offered to put their trust in you. Open up to them about your emotions, thoughts, and needs, allowing yourself to get close to them. Because you have a natural gift for getting people to like you, tell them how you feel about them and you will notice that you become less anxious and more grounded and comfortable in your own skin.

7. Type Seven: The Enthusiast

Growth for the enthusiast is achieved when you are no longer dependent on the highs of life because you will be able to pace yourself and immerse yourself into the real nature of existence which does include some lows. One way to do this is by observing your impulses and not giving into them; the more you resist, the more you will be able to focus on what is truly important.

When it comes to experiences, it is better to choose quality over quantity. Do not let yourself miss what is happening now because you were too busy anticipating the future. The present has a lot to teach you, unlike the future and as much as you wish, you will never be able to predict or completely prepare for anything.

Because you are a visionary, you should take opportunities that will allow you to think and generate new ideas. You will realize with time that doing this gives you joy, brings out social versions of yourself and you will actually discover a few talents.

8. Type Eight: The Challenger

As a type eight, you realize that you overvalue power and love to be in control of everything. However, if you are to grow, you need to come to the conclusion that true strength is in forgiveness because it is a stronger sign of courage. When in power, ensure that you act as a leader and not a boss; lead by example rather than just giving out orders. You will become a better communicator and worker for that matter.

As much as you think the world is against you, you should come to terms with the fact that they look up to you to set a bar. Believing that these people are against you, hurts your relationships because you end up alienating yourself from them. Identify the people who are on your side and let them know that you also care for them; this will not only improve your relationships but it will also give you a lot more self-confidence.

Positive affirmations that should govern your life include 'I can be gentle and strong at the same time', 'I extend a helping hand to those who need support', and 'I embrace every part of me, including my weaknesses'.

9. Type Nine: The Peacemaker

Though you may be used to daydreaming, growth means you remain in tune with people. Attempt to be more involved both mentally and physically so you can be an active member of society. It will improve your interpersonal skills and turn your relationships into opportunities for better communication.

In order to become more aware of your body and emotions, you should engage yourself in exercises. Not only is it a healthy way of forming self-discipline but it is also helping you increase your awareness of your feelings and emotions. Body-awareness will help you to concentrate and direct your attention in other parts of your life. It is also a great way to release stress and aggressions.

Hold positive affirmations such as being in touch with the world around you and working on your personal needs close to your heart. These will give you a surprisingly calm energy and help you understand that you do not need to lose yourself to others in order for you to be accepted, loved, or to simply keep the harmony.

Chapter Six: Enneagram and Relationships/Friendships

Relationships occupy a significant part of our time and attention and so they remain as one of the big mysteries in life. The enneagram can provide the archetype personalities for different individuals and suggests the pairings that are adequate with the potential advantages and issues that can come about with each pairing.

Enneagram Ones and Twos

The Ones and Twos are quite complementary as both provide each other an example of their qualities due to their attraction towards servicing roles and occupations. Their relationship is built on shared values, as they like to be on a path together. The enneagram Twos bring nurturing while the Ones do not easily allow themselves to relax. The Ones bring conscientiousness, consistency and integrity so they would not feel as though they have been abandoned. Now the trouble is that Twos may see the Ones as being unconcerned with others and not empathetic. They may feel like the Ones have idealistic ideals but do not have a lot of compassion for the real people.

The Two type enneagram can also pair with the Four which may result is a warm and passionate couple when both parties share their feelings in an open manner. They can be very good for each other as the Twos bring social skills and energy, which allows the Four to have confidence to interact very easily with other people. Type Fours brings a lot of creativity and have a good sense of humor. They also bring subtlety and emotional depth into the relationship through a sense of sensuality. On the flip side, the enneagram of Twos and Fours make better colleagues and friends than life partners. They both have a lot of needs which makes them cling to those who would respond to them adequately. Over the long term there can be competition for attention from one sector.

At the same time, the Twos can find the fours to be very moody and led by their impulses too much. They may also see a Four as being too hyper absorbed and hyper sensitive. On the other hand, the Four might see the Two as being too emotionally needy and desperate for other people to like them or seek them. They may be secretly envious though of the social abilities of the Two and the positive reactions they get from others though to the point they feel socially inept as they become intimidated. Being careful of these encounters and realizing them will bond a stronger connection.

Enneagram Type Three and Three
The type Three is a good pair with another Three as they bring an equal amount of effort to the table. They are both hard workers and always look for a way to improve their situation. They can therefore be very effective as a team, making them likely to be very successful in their endeavors. They are also very respectful of each other's privacy and would likely avoid drama within the relationship as they give space to each other to pursue their interests. The trouble with this union is one or both of the Threes might start feeling the relationship is taking time from their career and the pursuit towards success. One might feel that they are sacrificing their careers and potential for the sake of keeping the relationship together even though the other may be gaining mileage. This usually happens when the couple gets children and one spouse has to sacrifice their career to help out at home or when one travels and the other follows them in order to sacrifice.

Enneagram Type Four Goes with Type Five
Both the Fours and Fives bring particular richness and qualities to their development. The Fours may bring some artistry and emotional temperament as well as introspection and sensitivity in themselves. They are both private types and like depth as they do not mind taking the time to explore things to the full extent. The Fives bring an intellectual temperament as well as the habit of asking questions. Both of the types also bring a good sense of humor and love of the outlandish which can make the relationship

appear to be quirky and unique. The Fours help the Fives to remain in contact with themselves and their feelings as they have mutual tolerance for things that may come up and neither is shocked.

The trouble that comes with the pairing of the Four with the Five is the Four is an emotional type causing them to want more contact, which may result in too much demand. The Fives are thinking sorts and they may try for more space and detachment within the relationship which means they can become more private. The Fours may feel that the Fives are too intellectual or feel that the Fives are being too analytical towards the relationship rather than just being sympathetic with their emotional requirements and their situation. They might also have the feeling that the Fives are unavailable or uncaring to what they need. The Fives on the other hand look at it as the Four is a bottomless pit of needs that drain their time and energy. The Fives may also feel that the emotionality shows a lack of rationality or is a sign of immaturity. Speaking and opening up to one another is highly important for this pair.

Enneagram Type Ones and Sixes

Another pairing that would make a good team is the Ones and the Sixes and a lot of the time they are misidentified with each other. Both of the types can be very hard workers and have a strong sense of integrity and duty. Both of them care about the truth and being committed as they both want to serve other people and improve their world. Obviously they have the ability to bring other qualities which are their own. The Ones can bring a lot of mental clearness and rationality as they think very well when they are under pressure. They are also sure of themselves as compared to the Sixes. The Sixes on the other hand allow for warmth, better emotional response and generosity which can be endearing, making the Ones think again about their positions. The Sixes may have the chance to connect with people in a direct way as compared to the way the Ones tend to do. These qualities are quite attractive and they can make the couple a bit dynamic and yet a stable team. That is because they feel they can count on each other.

The trouble with this pairing is seen in the points of crises. As the level of stress continues to rise, the Ones can become judgmental of their partner and themselves. They may have the attitude of having all work and no play which seems they are a bit joyless and even difficult to be around. This enables resentment and accusations, allowing for a lot of bickering which can wear on the Sixes more than it would on a fellow One. If the tensions continue, then a Six would become more evasive and defensive as they will also want to stay away from their partner because they do not want conflict. To their misfortune, the Six is going to find it hard to talk in a direct manner concerning their fears and so there is not a lot which becomes aired out.

Enneagram Type Six and Three

This is not a common pairing but surprisingly these types can work as a team. The Threes bring a lot of energy and hard work to communicate and connect with individuals. This allows for unlimited potential for the relationship and for the personal growth of an individual. The Sixes can also bring compassion and a lot of quality comfort for the Threes that are experiencing stress. The Three may also pick up on the compassionate nature of the Sixes and then learn to open their hearts in a deeper way to those who are not as privileged.

Both of them have strong feelings of supporting each other towards goals, whether it is in finances or developing their talents. They both foster mutual levels of respect for the different traits each bring and the interests that they may invest within. The Three is also good for the Six's confidence building up their self-esteem. The Sixes may offer to support the Threes as well without them feeling smothered and this is important. Sixes may also assist the Threes to be a part of something which is greater than themselves like a church or a political organization and so they help them to see the big picture. On the flip side, they may also be able to bring out the worst attributes in each other if the relationship is not healthy. They are both competitive and can be workaholics as they both look externally for being reassured to make up for their secret insecurities. Both want to be socially accepted for the things they do and they like to avoid looking at their feelings or discussing their emotions. At the worst, both can be evasive and dishonest concerning their actions and the way they feel. They can deteriorate the partnership to the level it is at robotic functioning.

Enneagram Type Six and Eight

The type Sixes like to feel safe while the type Eights want to be the protective one and this is why they're a god pairing. One wants loyalty while the other gives it freely as their quality. The type Eight is also very focused and has a very intentional manner of being active and during this the Type Six can keep busy and try to not show how anxious they are. The type Eights are very impulsive before fully thinking things through and then weighing the consequences. The type Sixes on the other hand can be helpful to the Eights through looking at the worst case scenarios and the potential disadvantages and creation of backups. The type Sixes are skilled at the preparation for eventualities which may come up. Type Eights are direct about the people that they are and where they stand and this usually builds trust with the type Sixes. The Type Eights may learn to pay attention to the downside of their plans and try to manage them. The Type Sixes can excel in areas of research and bring some intellectual stimulation to the union between them and the Eights.

Enneagram Type Seven and Nine

These are one of the most often viewed pairings of the types as they bring a good mix of qualities. At the basic level, they are both positive perspective types that are upbeat about things and like to avoid anything negative in their lives. They are also both friendly and sociable, making them good with forgiveness and able to compromise to the best of their ability. On a social side, sevens are more active as compared to the nines and so they make the plans and have multiple interests. The sevens are also mentally fast and self-confident as they may be open to new experiences. The nines though bring support, steadiness and acceptance for the pairing. They are also more sympathetic and soft hearted as compared to the sevens. The trouble though is neither the nines nor the sevens are adept when it comes to working through painful elements in their relationship. Both of them prefer that things remain on the positive side. They tend to be both edgy and anxious when they are under stress and so they might take this out on each other rather than work things out as a couple. Between the two of them, the sevens are much more equipped to talk about what is bothering them as compared to the nines.

Bottom line

In order to individuate according to Carl Jung, there are some things that we can get for ourselves such as discipline, focus, containment and loyalty. These are all attributes that are attractive in getting a partner, however not every enneagram type has equal portions of the above. The main thing to note is you do not have to go for the enneagram matches that are advised in the text as you can build your traits to what you would like to be or what you think your essence is. You have to remember that your reactions are all about you one hundred percent of the time. Your partner is a good mirror for you to see yourself clearly because they are the representation of how you treat those closest to you.

Analyzing each personality type and the most compatible types will help you grow quicker and stronger. It is important to also remember that reading about the types isn't just for relationship purposes. This can immensely help you towards figuring out who you are and the best way you can live a more calming and fulfilled life, taking advantage of the traits in which you excel at.

Conclusion

Congratulations on finishing Enneagram. Hopefully you now have a better understanding of your personality type and those of others you know. Enneagram is a powerful guide towards finding your strengths and using them to your advantage as well as finding the strengths of others around you such as friends and family so you can use that to build your relationships with one another.

If you found this book helpful in anyway please leave a positive review on Amazon as it allows me to keep producing quality books. Thanks.

Below is a clear Table where you can do the Enneagram test to find your Personality Type!

							Type	9	6	3	1	4	2	8	5	7	
							Disagree	A	B	C	D	E	F	G	H	I	Agree
1	I have been imaginative and romantic.																
	I have been down to earth and pragmatic.																
2	I have a tendency to avoid confrontation.																
	I have a tendency to go into confrontations.																
3	I have usually been direct, idealistic and formal.																
	I have usually been diplomatic, ambitious and charming.																
4	I have tried to be intense and focused.																
	I have a tendency to be fun loving and spontaneous.																
5	I am a private person and have not tried to mi1 a lot with other people.																
	I have been hospitable as an individual and enjoyed welcoming																

		friends to my life.														
6	Generally, it has been hard to get a rise so to speak from me.															
	Generally, it has been easy to get a rise from me.															
7	I have been a high-minded idealist.															
	I have been more of a street-smart person or idealist.															
8	I have needed to give people affection.															
	I have had the preference of maintaining particular distance with individuals.															
9	I have needed to give people affection.															
	I have had the preference of maintaining particular distance with individuals.															
10	When given a chance at a new e1perience, I have asked myself whether I would enjoy it.															
	When presented with new e1periences I have asked mostly whether it would be useful to me.															
11	I have had the tendency of focusing too much on my needs.															
	I am one of those people that focuses mostly on other people.															

12	I come across as being too unsure of things and myself.															
	I give off the vibe that I am too sure of myself															
13	Other people have depended on the decisiveness and the strength that I give out.															
	Other people have depended on the knowledge and insight that I give out.															
14	I tend to be more goal oriented as opposed to being relationship oriented.															
	I tend to be more relationship oriented than goal oriented.															
15	I am not very able to speak up for myself.															
	I am very outspoken and so I have said what others have wished that they had the nerve to say.															
16	It is difficult for me to become more fle1ible and to take things easier.															
	It has been hard for me to stop alternatives and to do something which is definite.															
17	I have a tendency for procrastination and to be hesitant.															
	I have a tendency for being domineering and being courageous.															
18	My eagerness to have others depend on me has severally gotten me in trouble with them.															

	My hesitation to get involved a lot has gotten me into trouble with other people.																	
19	Usually, I have had the ability to put feelings aside and to get the task at hand done.																	
	Usually, I have had to work through my emotions before I could get things done.																	
20	Usually, I am adventurous and have taken risks.																	
	Usually I am quite meticulous and cautious.																	
21	I have had tendencies to be serious as a reserved person that likes to discuss things.																	
	I have tended to be supporting as a giving person that likes the company of other people.																	
22	I have usually felt the need to perform in the right manner.																	
	I have often gotten the need to be a pillar of stability.																	
23	I have been interested usually in the maintenance of stability and peace.																	
	I have been interested usually in asking tough queries while maintaining some independence.																	
24	I am very soft hearted and sentimental.																	
	I am skeptical and hard-nosed in thought processes.																	

25	I have worried a lot that if I let my guard down that other people are going to take advantage.																		
	I have worried that I am missing out on connections with other people.																		
26	My habit of telling others what to do is annoying to my loved ones.																		
	My habit of being isolated has put others off.																		
27	Usually when troubles have gotten the best of me, I have treated myself to relieve the stress.																		
	Usually when troubles have gotten to me, I have been able to work and eventually tune them out.																		
28	I have not depended on individuals as I have done things solely by myself.																		
	I have depended on friends and they have known they have the ability to depend on me.																		
29	I have had the tendency to be self-absorbed and moody.																		
	I have tendencies to be detached and preoccupied.																		
30	I like to comfort others when they are distressed and calm them down.																		
	I like to challenge other people and to shake them up.																		
31	I have been a serious and earnest or self-disciplined individual.																		
	I have been a serious a																		

	carefree and sociable individual.
32	I have liked to let people know about my strengths or what I can do well.
	I have been very shy about telling others about my strengths and abilities.
33	Having comfort and security is more important to me as compared to pursuing personal interests and preferences.
	Pursuing personal interests has been more significant than having comfort or security.
34	When I have had conflict with other people, I back down on rare occasions.
	When I have had conflict with other individuals, I tended to back down or withdraw.
35	I have been known for my sense of humor and unsinkable optimistic attitude.
	I have been known for my quiet strength and e1ceptional amount of generosity as an individual.
36	A lot of success has been because of talent in making a good impression
	A lot of success has been attained despite the lack of interest in development of interpersonal skills.

Total									
Column	A	B	C	D	E	F	G	H	I
Type	9	6	3	1	4	2	8	5	7

Whatever column has the highest number represents what personality type you are!

www.ingramcontent.com/pod-product-compliance
Lightning Source LLC
Chambersburg PA
CBHW071912290426
44110CB00013B/1365